D0305295

LAURA DAVIES

NATURALLY . . .

LAURA DAVIES

NATURALLY . . .

with Lewine Mair

BLOOMSBURY

The information in this book was correct to the best of the editor's and
publisher's belief at the time of going to press. While no responsibility can be
accepted for errors and omissions, the editor and publisher would welcome
corrections and suggestions for material to include in subsequent editions of
this book.

This edition first published in 1996 by
Bloomsbury Publishing Plc
2 Soho Square
London, W1V 6HB

ISBN 0 7475 2764 4
10 9 8 7 6 5 4 3 2 1

Typeset by Hewer Text Composition Services, Edinburgh
Printed and bound in Great Britain by Clays Ltd, St Ives plc

CONTENTS

FOREWORD

I had heard all about Laura, long before she, Jack Nicklaus and myself got together to play in the Wendy's Three-Tour Challenge at Muirfield Village just before Christmas 1995. For as long as I can remember, people had been telling me that the American women's tour had their own John Daly; that Laura Davies was my opposite number in terms of launching a long ball.

I had expected her to hit a bigger ball than the rest of the lady professionals, but I have to admit that I wasn't entirely prepared for the monumental crack she gives it. I can tell you that there were several occasions when Jack and I exchanged looks as her drives soared into the distance.

Nor was I expecting Laura to have as good a short game as she has. Her touch is great, and that, as much as anything, was why we had such a closely-contested match at Muirfield Village.

So, I had fun watching her and I also had fun talking with her about golf on our respective tours. The women are lucky to have such a warm personality in their midst. I hope she will continue to brighten the scene for a long time to come. Also, I'm looking forward to the day we can play together in the JCPenney mixed event at the end of the season.

We could go a long way in the tournament as well as off the tee.

John Daly

Chapter 1

Further along Life's Fairway

Speak to any of the rookie professionals on either the American Ladies' Professional Golf Association tour or its opposite number in Europe, and they will almost certainly tell you that they plan on playing the women's tour for ten years, maximum. After that, they will be settling down and having a family.

It seldom works that way. As often as not, the golfers get hooked on their lifestyle and cannot bring themselves willingly to declare their tournament innings closed.

I understand how it happens and I understand, too, the extent of my own addiction. When, like me, you have played 12 straight years on tour, it's impossible to turn your back on it all. So much of your life is out there. . . . In a sense, it's where you belong. Even when I take a week off, I find that I am forever switching on Ceefax to see how my friends are doing.

In ten years' time, I would like to think that I will have cut down on my tournament appearances to around the 15 a year mark. That, as I look at it today, would be quite enough to let me to stay in touch and, at the same time, would allow me to build on other aspects of my career, such as course design.

I feel guilty about asking just too much of a life which, to date, has treated me ridiculously well, but I would like to be playing those 15 tournaments with a family in tow – a husband and two children. There would be one boy and one girl, both of whom would be as nuts on sport as I am myself. They wouldn't have any alternative because, apart from anything else, I have always been convinced that sport is the best antidote to trouble-making among the young.

Not long ago, people were appalled to read in an article in *Golf World* magazine that I had denigrated my appearance and said of my chances of marriage, 'Who would have me?' I must confess that it is exactly the kind of hasty reply I am apt to give when the conversation turns to any subject bordering on the embarrassing.

I suppose you could say that I have my admirers. Shy though I am, I doubt it can do any harm to air the story – it's one which has grown a little in the telling – of how I was asked out by one of the tournament officials not long after I had joined the European tour. He had sought advice from someone who had been around the tour for rather longer than he had himself, and the advice he had been given was that he should suggest morning coffee rather than dinner. The theory was that anything more would frighten the life out of me.

He heeded that counselling up to a point, opting for something in between – lunch. My reaction, so it is said, was a panic-stricken 'Brilliant idea; let's all go.' Anyway, we all went. The tournament official, myself, a handful of caddies and a couple of Australian friends.

Today, there is the ongoing tale of Henry Lee, a wealthy Korean-born Canadian who, for some reason, became besotted with me after watching the Du Maurier a few years ago. Henry, a retired surgeon, watches most of my major tournaments and smiles, proprietorially, at every good shot. He writes letters on much the same lengthy scale as a good tee shot and, to my horror, laces them with proposals of marriage. On one occasion, he was bold enough to include a copy of his divorce papers. I have never written back, though my dad, Dave, has once or twice been moved to tell him that he is wasting his time. There was one occasion when Henry interrupted my dad's Sunday lunch to ask, 'Is it true, Laura's getting married?'

My father replied in the negative before telling him that the answer was not one to make an iota of difference to him either way. 'Why don't you look for someone your own age?' came Davies Snr's suggestion.

This did not go down well with Henry, who replied with an oblique 'So, you don't believe in mixed marriages.'

At the end of the 1994 US Open, Henry was tugging at my sleeve and asking if he should fly over to London to watch me playing in the Weetabix British Women's Open of that year. I told him, in no uncertain terms, that he would do better to save his money. As luck would have it, he put the wrong interpretation on that comment. He thought that I was suggesting he should save for our future together.

More letters followed, but by then the press had cottoned on to what he was about. After a reluctant appearance on Canadian television, Henry retreated. Or so it seemed. I was hugely relieved but, on the first day of the 1995 Nabisco Dinah Shore at Palm Springs, he was back.

'Have you found yourself a wife yet, Henry?' asked one of the journalists, a little mischievously.

'No,' replied Lee.

'Are you still after Laura?'

'I guess so,' he returned, his face at once sheepish and smiling.

By the time of the 1995 Du Maurier, a new stream of correspondence had caused more alarm than amusement. In one of the notes, his punch-line was something of a conversation-stopper: 'If I can't have you, no one else will.'

That was the moment when Dad decided to pass on the information to Charlie Mechem, then the Chief Executive of the LPGA tour. Mechem, in turn, put the matter in the hands of the FBI. They stopped Henry coming to an end-of-season tournament in Seattle, escorting him back to his hotel and waiting as he packed.

Again, they had him arrested in March 1996 when he turned up at Tucson. He was dragged, shouting, from the course. That made me a little nervous, as did the suggestion from the FBI that if anyone was at risk from this obsessive individual, it was those around me. As the FBI said, Lee was under the impression that it was others who were poisoning my mind against him.

For myself, I have never seen any point in adding to the drama. When asked about it, I merely repeat what I have said all along. 'I don't want to hurt Dr Lee's feelings, but he clearly isn't the man for me.'

So, who would be the right man?

The main requisites are that the chap in question should have a sense of humour, that he should know how to enjoy himself, and that he should enjoy spending money. Furthermore he would have to be a good friend. He would also need to love sport but, preferably, he would not be a professional golfer. If he were, we'd never see each other.

Mind you, if I were pressed to give an example of my kind of man, I would have to plump for Freddie Couples, even though he is a professional. Fred, of course, is happily accounted for, but he is good-looking, wonderfully natural and a lot of fun to be around. (We played together in the Wendy's Three-Tour Challenge at the end of 1994 – a competition involving the American senior tour, the men's regular tour and the women's circuit. Patty Sheehan and Nancy Lopez were the others involved as our side finished joint second with the seniors.)

In a more serious vein, I accept that I am not too well placed to find this man of my dreams.

One of the down sides of my life is the way you are never in the same place for more than a week at a time. Tucson one week, Phoenix the next, Palm Springs the week after . . . and so it goes on.

I have known players who went on to marry men they met in pro-ams. Barb Bunkowski was one; Donna Andrews, the 1994 US Open champion, another.

The trouble is that I do not have the brand of confidence which goes with meeting someone one day and accepting a date that same evening. I'm just not like that. I would need to know someone well. All my friends are people I have got to know gradually across the years. I'm the last person for hurriedly forged friendships. In other words, any prospective husband would more likely come from the ranks of those already on or around the golf scene.

When, in ten years' time, I have weaned myself off the busy schedule I have at the moment, I doubt I will miss the travel or the endless round of hotel rooms anything like as much as I will miss my friends. It is not that I dislike hotel rooms. In fact, I love coming back at the end of a day's golf to an apartment which has been tidied by someone else, while I often chuckle to myself at the way in which my bedroom at home could so easily be mistaken for a hotel apartment.

Though, as I have implied earlier, there are professionals who come to see the tour as 'home', I thank heaven that I am not among them.

My house at Ottershaw, Surrey, means a lot to me. I share it with my mother, Rita, and my stepfather, Mike Allen, in an arrangement which works wonderfully well for all of us. I long to get back there after two or three weeks away.

We found it in the winter of 1994–95 at a time when I had 'itchy feet' and felt the need for a property with some land, which we did not have at our old cottage in the heart of the village.

I had heard that Northwood House was up for sale some months before and had driven up to the gates just to have a look. I liked what I saw – a mass of tangled land with a pretty house above – but I felt that at £450,000, it was beyond my means, even though Mum and Uncle Mike were going to be paying their share.

Some months later, after a successful run in the States which included wins in the Standard Register Ping tournament in Phoenix, the Sara Lee Classic and the McDonald's, I rang home from a tournament in France, the Evian Masters. During the course of conversation, Mum volunteered that she had suddenly had the urge to go and look round the inside. As she started on a litany of the property's good points, including a snooker room and five acres of land, I cut her off in mid-stream. 'Buy it!' I said, impulsively.

'Let's wait till you've had a look when you get back,' she advised.

I finished tenth in the Evian and, after flying home on the Sunday, went that night to have a peep through the windows. I knew at once that this was precisely what we wanted. We made an offer the following day and, later in the week, upped it by £10,000. At that, it was ours. We moved in that August, on the Monday after the 1994 British Women's Open at Woburn.

No sooner were we installed, with the dogs tearing around after rabbits, than I was making plans for a tennis court, a properly maintained golf green, a swimming pool and a football pitch. Sport occupies most of my spare time and always will, though whether I will still be using the football pitch when I am in my forties and fifties is another matter.

I am conscious of the fact that I have friends who make more selfless use of their weeks away from the tour. Alison Nicholas, my Solheim Cup partner, is involved in Christians in Sport. When she and Betsy King, the former American Open champion, come off a four-tournament stint and head for some distant corner of the world to help with orphans in Romania or some equally worthy cause, I feel admiration tinged with envy. I love children and I think to myself that I would like to do that but, when the moment comes and it's a matter of heading for Romania or home, I choose home every time. It doesn't sound good, but I'd sooner be kicking a ball around.

I'm selfish with my time, if you like, but, against that, I do need to relax. Contrary to the opinion of so many I come across, playing tournament golf is no tea-party.*

Gambling is another favourite pastime and one which, I suspect, will keep me happily occupied when my golf takes a back seat. Blame my grandmother! I learned at her knee when the two of us would sit ourselves down every Saturday to watch the horses on television.

I bet heavily; very heavily by some standards, but I can put my hand on my heart and say there has only been the one time when I have broken my own rule of never betting more than I am prepared to lose.

It happened in London in 1994. I walked out of the casino having lost £4,000 when the limit I had set myself was £3,000. I was cross. I knew I had gone too far. It was obscene to have lost that amount of money in a world where so many are struggling. Not, mind you, that I think it exactly laudable to lose £3,000.

One February day, at the start of 1995, I placed a £20 bet known as a Canadian, a combination bet involving three horses and a couple of dogs. All five won, and that night I collected a little matter of £27,691 and 34p. Two days later, I won £6,000 on a football bet and I have to say that it worried me that I felt nothing – no thrill whatever.

* LM: On the same day that Laura talked about having been selfish with her time, one had been struck by how much more she gives of herself than most players to those who come to watch the women's game.

Where people were hesitating to ask some of the more poker-faced professionals if they could take photographs, no one hesitated to ask Laura. Her smile was in place already; it was simply a matter of pressing the camera shutter. On the same tack, when she hits one of her massive tee shots, she is never remotely lordly about it. She revels in the crowd's amused astonishment. 'She may be shy,' says her father, Dave, 'but she's always loved entertaining people.'

Charlie Mechem, the LPGA's erstwhile Chief Executive and a man who is held in the highest regard by everyone in the golf community, raised his eyebrows when he heard of Laura's suggestion that she was selfish.

'Laura,' he opined, 'is as accessible and outgoing as any superstar I've ever met.'

Earlier that week, he had been having a meeting with prospective sponsors who had told him that they had been struck by the extent to which Laura had interacted with the crowds and happily given autographs at a time when she could have been keeping out of the way.

The point Mechem wanted to make was that Laura was giving of herself all the while. What is more, he had the feeling that she might one day follow in the footsteps of another retired woman professional of his acquaintance. Once the player in question at last had some time to herself, she wanted nothing so much as to give of it to others.

So how do I make out at the end of a gambling year?

Last year, with that big win, I finished up ahead, but if you look back over my professional career, the story is a little different.

Before I go on, let me spell out that I have never indulged in an expensive hobby like sailing. Nor have I wasted my money on cigarettes or alcohol. I gamble because I find it fun and because it seldom bothers me if I lose. I have some wonderful evenings up at the Ritz, chatting with old friends before we get down to business.

Now for the answer. I have maybe lost half a million in the last 12 years. Pounds, that is.

Chapter 2

Formative Golfing Years

There is no question that my brother, Tony, has been the biggest influence on my golfing life. When Tony, at ten, was given his first bag of clubs, I was placated with a five iron. Since I was three years younger, that was held to be enough.

My father remembers taking us, early on, to play on a public course at Corby in Leicestershire. He says that I would grab the club half-way down the shaft, rather as I would do in the 1980s, and that I belted the ball as hard as I could. He used to take home movies of the two of us, and he was always struck by the fact that Tony's swing was very good. He said that I seemed to do all the right things, too, but that he didn't, for a moment, think he had a champion on his hands.

My dad used to say that the worst thing that can happen to a Davies was to be beaten by another Davies and, before too many years had passed, Tony and I were involved in regular games which brought out the best and the worst in us. We hated to lose to each other. Out of sight of the members, we would chuck clubs, argue with each other and generally behave as you never could if you were playing with anyone else. I don't know how we got away with it.

I played at Guildford before joining West Byfleet, the club where I still have so many links. The reason I moved was because

West Byfleet was within a bicycle ride of the family home and not – as some have had it – because there was any difference of opinion with the ladies at Guildford. In fact, I remember them with great affection. However, there was one incident which maybe served to fuel a rumour or two – namely, my winning of the ladies' medal. I was waiting, with bated breath, to be handed the little silver spoon for what was the lowest net score.

To my chagrin, a club official said there would be no spoon. I was a junior member rather than one paying the full subscription and, as such, I was not entitled to make off with any of the silverware.

By the time Mum arrived at the club to fetch me, the tears had started to flow.

'Did you have a bad day?' she asked, concerned.

'I won the medal,' I replied, between sobs, 'but they wouldn't give me my spoon.'

No one is more ready to seize on an injustice than Mum, and she marched into the clubhouse to bat on my behalf.

'Laura will be having her spoon,' she said, or words to that effect.

The prized piece of cutlery was duly handed over and that was the end of the matter.

More than fifteen years later, there are still a number of clubs who persist in refusing to allow juniors to win prizes. Officialdom, however, has found an excellent way of hitting back. The English Ladies' Golf Association, for example, has decreed that those clubs who put petty restrictions on their junior members will not be allowed to participate in some of ELGA's special club events. This is a very good move, because it is madness not to give every encouragement possible to girl golfers, especially when everyone complains that they are in short supply. If women in golf clubs do not go out of their way to make them feel at home, they will be doubly inclined to give golf a miss and try their hand at tennis or some other sport.

Though, at the outset of my professional career, I was hardly noted for too many lengthy stints on the practice ground, I used to put in more work than most when I was in my teens. During school holidays, Mum would drop me off at the club and I would work all day, pausing for no longer than it took to pour my lunch money into the fruit machine. Even at 14, when I was hacking around off a 20 handicap, I knew that I wanted to be a good golfer, although I had no conception that it was a game from which I might one day earn a living.

The truth was that I was mad about all sports. I represented Fullbrook school, Weybridge, at almost every level in netball, hockey, tennis and rounders but, to my continuing irritation, was never given my colours at any of them. Today, I do not mind giving my version of why that was.

One summer's day, when I was itching to play someone at something, I made the mistake of challenging a PE teacher to a game of tennis. I compounded this tactical error by winning the match 6–0, 6–0. As far as I was concerned, this was simply one more good result under my belt.

When the day came for the presentation of colours to the fifth form, I was filled with eager anticipation. My friends told me that I was certain to get mine, and I was quietly confident. Mr Smyth, the headmaster, began to read out the list of names in alphabetical order. When it came to the Ds, I put a foot forward as I heard the first syllable of my christian name. Then I checked, reddened, and melted back into the line. The head was calling for my friend, Lorna Didsbury.

The rest of the class, in endeavouring to cheer me up at morning break, wasted no time in deciding where I had gone wrong. They said I should never have beaten the teacher.

I was gutted then and, crazy though it sounds, I'm still gutted now. The hurt went very deep. So deep that I have never gone back to Fullbrook, even though I have been asked on two or three occasions.

Someone pointed out to me how the politician Nicholas Soames got awarded his cricket colours 36 years after he had left his preparatory school, but I'm not looking for anything like that. In his case, the inference was that he hadn't been much good at cricket at the time and that the colours were being awarded 'for subsequent achievements'.

I sat five or six O levels and failed the lot. I was not remotely academic, but I suspect that things might have been rather different had I been able to take those subjects which interested me. Subjects like cricket, tennis, golf and gambling . . .

Mr Smyth, who had no doubt sussed from my 'streetwise' qualities that I was maybe a little smarter than I would have them believe, tried to make me see what he saw as sense. When I said I wanted a career in golf, he was quick to warn, 'You're going to have to get a proper job.'

Yet, when it was clear that my mind was made up, Mr Smyth was far from unhelpful, allowing me to devote my 'work experience' period to golf.

By this time I had improved to the point where there could have been a problem in finding appropriate opposition, but he had just the man: the school truancy officer, a gentleman with whom, incidentally, I had had no prior dealings.

I left school at the end of that O level year and thereafter complemented summer golf with a variety of winter jobs . . . as a petrol pump attendant, a clerk at Corals and a checkout girl in a supermarket. I have no regrets about not having made more of my education, my feeling being that if I had stayed on at school and sat my exams again, I might never have got off to the same good start in golf.

I received a magnificent grounding in the Surrey county arena, where the players of the moment included Jill Thornhill, the 1983 British champion; Diane Bailey, three times captain of the Curtis Cup team; Winnie Wooldridge, who played for Scotland both at golf and tennis and twice reached the quarter-finals at Wimbledon; Jill Nicholson, the former British Girls' champion; and Catherine Bailey, who would become quite a force in the realm of Senior women's golf.

Along with Joan Rothschild, a Surrey vice-president, these great players kept me in line. They were what I would call 'constructively bossy'. I sometimes got fed up with them telling me to tidy myself up and get my hair cut but, over the years, I came to see that most of what they were saying was right. Golf is a game in which standards have to be maintained.

Surrey turned me from a pretty useless amateur into a player who had a very much better idea of what she was about. Jill Thornhill, in particular, showed me how to practise more effectively and instilled in me the rudiments of course management.

I made my debut for England in the 1983 European Junior Team championships in Holland where, extraordinarily enough, my opponent on the last afternoon against Sweden was none other than Lotta Neumann. Today, when I look at the photo taken of us standing side by side on that Dutch trip, I often wonder what odds I would have got against our winning the US Open in successive years.

Going back to the match, I can remember that we were playing second in the last afternoon line-up behind Penny Grice, now Penny Grice-Whittaker, and Helen Alfredsson. At that moment when Penny defeated Alfredsson on the 14th green, my game was still poised to go either way but, buoyed by Penny's result, I stepped up a gear to notch three successive birdies and a 2 and 1 win. England, who had drawn the foursomes 2–2, went on to win this prestigious European title 4½–2½. Nothing could have been more fun.

In penning her report, Liz Boatman, the England captain, wrote of me that I was 'definitely a gallery player . . . Her great potential in terms of length should not be ignored.'

That week may have been special, but there was better to come, when I was chosen for the 1984 Curtis Cup at Muirfield. That was the nail-biter of a contest which just finished in the Americans' favour but proved the springboard for successive Great Britain and Ireland wins in 1986 and 1988.

Having lost in the first morning's foursomes, I did not come in again until the last singles series, in which I holed downhill from ten feet on the 18th green to defeat Anne Sander.

Since I had reached the last green with a drive and eight iron to my opponent's drive and three wood, she was apparently sufficiently shaken to decide on a complete change of swing – even though she was 46. Back in the States, her coach predicted that she could not expect to reap the rewards till she was 50. He was not too far out – Anne was 52 when she returned for a 1990 Curtis Cup at Somerset Hills, which the Americans won with room to spare. (Anne bagged two points from two starts.)

Since I managed to win the 1984 English Intermediate title, I felt I had the necessary credentials to turn professional at the beginning of 1985. My mum and Uncle Mike gave me £1,000 to help me to get started.

My first tournament was the Ford Classic on the Duke's Course at Woburn. I found myself paired with two Scots, Dale Reid and Jane Connachan. None of us was exactly on song and, when I had a second-round 85, I was fully prepared to miss the cut. Indeed, Tony, who had agreed to caddie for me, had already returned home. Not until later did I understand why he had made such a quick exit. While I had dipped into my £1,000 to pay for accommodation, Tony had spent the night freezing in his car.

Fortunately, our home was not far away, and we managed to get our act together and finish with two acceptable scores.

On to the Hennessy tournament in France, to which the great Jan Stephenson had been invited. I played unbelievably well for someone only in her second tournament, but the press did not take too long to work out that something had gone badly wrong. They had called me in to talk about my good week, but when I arrived in the press room I was in tears.

The story, which would make the front page of some papers, gradually came out. There was a big drive on at that time concerning the players' appearance, and Colin Snape, then Executive Director of the Women's European Tour, had made it clear that anyone wearing jeans would be fined. I was not wearing jeans, but the colour of my cotton slacks was not too far removed from that of jeans. To Snape, they were as a red rag to a bull and, when one of the girls drew his attention to them, he had no hesitation in fining me £50. The wording of his complaint was that I was bringing the tour into disrepute.

What hurt me as much as anything was the fact that I did not at the time have any smart clothes. The only money I had to my name was the aforementioned £1,000 and, with a whole season ahead of me, I had not felt inclined to blow it on new gear.

No sooner had I left the press room than a major row began to break out between those who felt that Snape had done entirely the right thing and those who believed that nothing could have been more unjust.

In a move which hardly helped to cement the relationship between Snape and Giles Hennessy, the sponsor, one of the journalists went up to Hennessy to ask what he had thought of my appearance. 'She looked charming, to me' is what the gallant Frenchman said.

Then, the same journalist tackled Jan Stephenson, who had won the tournament. Jan has always been among the most dashingly glamorous of the women golfers and, though she has a hard side to her, the issue was one which brought out her softer self. She appreciated that it had to be difficult for someone like me to find trousers which were a perfect fit. The comments she made for press purposes were along the lines that it was wicked that I should have found myself in such trouble on a day when I should have been receiving nothing but pats on the back for having done so well.

Both in the car and on the boat back, I could think of nothing except that fine. As Jan had said, what should have been among the happiest afternoons of my life had been turned into a nightmare.

On the plus side, my sorry plight seemed to win me the beginnings of the support I am lucky enough to have enjoyed all my professional golfing days. What's more, my prize money enabled me to repay my mum and Uncle Mike and to revel in the heady sensation that I was up and running.

Chapter 3

A Family Business

At the time I won the US Open in 1987, I was managed by Colin Snape, the former Executive Director of the Women's European Tour. Some people found it difficult to comprehend, because he was the man who, at the start of 1985, fined me £50 for contravening the tour's dress rules. As it turned out, I had subsequently developed a good relationship with him.

Mark McCormack's International Management Group made their approach after the US Open. What appealed to me most about what they had to offer was a three-year contract with the Weetabix organization.

Since Snape had instigated the Maruman club and clothing contract I still have today, I followed IMG's advice in buying myself out of my player-manager arrangement. After that, I put myself wholly in IMG's hands. They were, after all, the management company of the moment, with many of the biggest names in sport playing from their stable.

It may sound strange, but in six or so years I was with IMG, I never met Mark McCormack, except for one occasion when he introduced himself to me on the 1st tee at Pine Isle during a pro-am. There was an invitation to a Mark McCormack party in the early 1990s but, at least in my eyes, it came a bit late. I turned it down.

I am the first to say that IMG are 'the tops' for those whom they view as their foremost clients. In truth, there were times when I felt myself to be a part of that elite corps. Equally, there were times when I felt they had forgotten about me altogether. 'Fair weather managers' is maybe the best way of getting across the manner in which their interest would plummet when I was going through a lean spell.

It was in the leaner times that I felt I needed them most. I was obviously not expecting them to ring with lucrative exhibition offers and the like, but I would have welcomed the odd 'caring' phone call. It would have suggested that they were as interested in me as a person rather than merely as a money-making golfer.

I would like to emphasize that I exclude IMG Japan from any criticisms, for they are a crack team. IMG's personal service in these islands and in many another part of the world is, however, virtually non-existent.

There was the odd occasion when I would turn up at a hotel and the receptionists would deny all knowledge of any booking in my name. Let me tell you of the night I arrived at the Doubletree Hotel, Tucson, after playing in a tournament in some other part of the USA. It was not the most appealing of trips – just a one-night, one-day affair for the press conference I had to do for the Tucson Classic which I had won the previous year. The only consolation was that IMG had assured me that everything was arranged.

By the time I arrived at my destination, it was one o'clock in the morning. I was dying to get to my bed but, when I gave my name to the receptionist, she just looked at me blankly and said I would have to go somewhere else. It took me at least an hour to persuade her to give me a room.

There were journeys as unpredictable as some of my early rounds of golf, while I have to say I felt particularly sore about the way in which IMG would apparently book me on the first flight which came to light rather than look for a more economic alternative. It was my money they were spending and, rightly or wrongly, it was my impression that they were less concerned about saving me a few hundred pounds than saving themselves a bit of time.

Along with my mother, I worked out how much IMG were making from me per month – it was 25 per cent of every deal and 10 per cent of all prize money – and decided that it was madness.

I was returning from the US Open at Oakmont in 1992, the championship won by Patty Sheehan from Juli Inkster in an 18-hole play-off, when I first began to toy with the notion of a different way ahead. Tony, the older brother with whom I had first started to play golf, had been caddying for me for five years and, sister-brother relationships being what they are, we had long before accepted that the arrangement could not last for ever.

Five years earlier, we had won the *1987 US Open* together in a week when my then regular caddie, Tim Clark, must have been going through the tortures of the damned at home. After that, we had gone on to win many another tournament besides. But I did not always react well to Tony's advice . . . If, for instance, I had a bad hole and embarked on one of my rushing fits, the last thing I wanted was for him to tell me to slow down. Everyone used to laugh at the way in which Tony would adopt a totally dead-pan expression, one which could not possibly spark anything in the way of sisterly irritation.

There was one off-course argument – about what, I cannot remember – in which I came close to knocking him out cold. By way of completing the job, I threw his bedclothes out of the hotel window on to the cars below.

To sum up, we're very close; we argue a lot. What brother and sister don't?

On that journey back from Oakmont in 1992 I asked Tony if he would switch from caddie to manager, and he accepted.

The following week, at the Weetabix British Open, we met with an IMG executive. I explained that while I still valued my IMG connection, I wanted Tony to take charge of my personal arrangements. The IMG man said that Tony was not qualified to fill such a role and that he would not know what he was doing. We chose to ignore such warnings. Today, I have the best of both worlds as Tony works happily in conjuction with the people I like the most from Mark McCormack's empire.

As a personal manager, Tony could not be more thorough. He doesn't just check a hotel booking once. More often than not, he will check it three times and, touch wood, nothing has gone wrong in two and a half years. The organizational side of things is his forte, but he also negotiates contracts and sifts through the many invitations and offers. When I was managed solely by IMG, I always had the feeling that there were all sorts of possibilities which I never heard about on the grounds that the people involved were unable to talk the right kind of figures. The system now is that Tony will run everything past me and, if some less lucrative venture takes my fancy, I will involve myself, regardless. My column in *Women and Golf* magazine is a case in point.

I enjoy having this opportunity to interact with some of those who are good enough to take an interest in my golf. For instance, there was one lady who was disappointed in the manner in which I appeared to lose heart at the end of my single in the 1994 Solheim Cup at The Greenbrier. After reading what she had to say on the letters page, I got scribbling right away. I liked being in a position to explain my side of the story in my column. For the record, my explanation was along the lines that the team side of things had consumed me to such an extent that I could not muster any great enthusiasm for salvaging shreds of glory on an individual basis.

As Tony took over on the business front, so Mark Fulcher took over as caddie. I would not want this to go to his head, but Mark is a thoroughly engaging fellow. He mustered his share of O and A levels, which is more than I ever did, but he could see no point in working in an office when he could be travelling Europe with a golf-bag on his back. Having for some time been taking a metaphorical battering from Florence Descampe, the tempestuous but undeniably talented Belgian who played in the 1992 Solheim Cup, he was ready for a new employer. (In fact he went back to working for Florence in 1995 and was still with her through the early months of her first pregnancy in 1996.)

Mark and I had known each other a long time and we got off on the right foot. We were united in the belief that I should put in a bit of extra work on and around the putting green. Together, we won tournaments all over the world.

Our friendship is intact to this day, with each of us describing the other as a 'best friend'. However, our caddie-player relationship foundered midway through 1994. 'Lots of little things,' is how I explain the split when anyone asks.*

My cousin, Matthew Adams, who had been caught up in the same world through caddying for one of the Japanese contingent, accepted my suggestion that he carry the bag. In fact, he was only too happy to oblige. In 1994, my first year of winning over a million dollars, he pocketed a little matter of $100,000. Now he drives a BMW.

I cannot remember any time in my life when Matthew was not a part of my golf career. He was at Plainfield in 1987 when he came away with a lump on his chest of 1.68 proportions after being hit by one of my tee shots at the 18th. Seconds earlier, he had been exhorting a new-found friend to see how far his cousin could hit the ball.**

Though, initially, I wondered if my fun-loving cousin might take the job a little lightly, it was soon apparent that he was

---

* **LM:** Try as he might, Fulcher could not stop boasting about Laura's prowess and, when Laura heard snatches of what he had been saying, she winced.

The most unassuming of golfers, she did her best to explain that such talk would breed resentment and that it was better to leave her clubs to do the talking. Mark accepted what she was saying but did not find it any easier to contain himself. Thus, when more instances of his extolling her golfing virtues came to light, the break-up was inevitable. 'Basically,' he said, 'I blew it. I had the best bag in the world and I let it go.'

** **Dave Davies:** We were staying in this ridiculously expensive hotel for the Open at Plainfield. Everyone had left it to me to do the booking and, by the time I got round to it, this was the only one I could get.

The bills were getting bigger and bigger as the tournament was delayed first for rain and then for Laura's play-off with JoAnne Carner and Ayako Okamoto.

It was the night before the play-off that I remember the best. Laura, for prepared to give it his all. During a tournament, he's probably the first to go to bed if we have an early tee-off time.

Whereas, with Tony, an untimely comment from either of us would pave the way for a lingering atmosphere, my exchanges with Matthew tend not to spawn any lasting ill feeling. Either of us can say 'Shut up!' to the other without any repercussions.

I like having a close relative at my side when I am travelling the circuit. Some do not mind going places on their own, but I would be miserable. I need that kind of company. For instance, though I do not mind having breakfast on my own, I would never go down to dinner without a friend. I hate to see someone sitting on their own at that hour; it strikes me as sad. Sooner than do that, I would order room service.

The other thing about having someone with you is that the tour can be a dangerous place. There has been more than one case of a player being accosted on the walk from car to motel room.

Because of the way it left me with family on both sides of the Atlantic, I suppose I could claim that I have been more a beneficiary than a victim of the break-up of my parents' marriage, painful though it was at the time. As a family, we moved to Marietta, Georgia, in 1967 when my father, Dave, was offered a job as a design engineer for Lockhead. I was three at the time. The split came three years later and my mother, Tony and I moved back to England. Mum eventually married Mike Allen, whom I have often described as the best stepfather anyone could have. He is my No. 1 fan in these islands, never missing a shot. If Mum starts chatting with anyone, he is apt to nip ahead and watch on his own.

some reason – or more likely no reason – was embroiled in a pillow fight with Matthew. I barked, 'Cut that out or you'll break a finger.'

They did not appear to take any notice but, ten minutes later, Laura, feigning tears, showed me a limp-looking digit and said, 'Dad, you were right . . . I have broken my finger.'

My heart had sunk to the depths, and I was just embarking on the 'What did I tell you' bit when there was a ripple of giggles from the two of them.

Dad, now retired and living in South Carolina, saw me win my US Open. He even managed to catch the last hole of the play-off where the crowds were enormous and most people were complaining that they could not see a thing. A friendly photographer had handed him his armband and ushered him inside the ropes.

A steward saw what had happened and told him that he would have to get out. Even when Dad explained, gently, that his daughter was playing, the steward would have none of it. 'Good try, buddy!' is all he said before making another attempt to evict him. Finally, one of the USGA people stepped in and confirmed that Dad was my father and that he was to let him in.

Today, he attends around eight of my American tournaments each year. More often than not, I will seek him out between the green and the tee, especially when I am looking to celebrate the holing of a birdie putt.

He was over in Dalmahoy to watch our Solheim Cup win in 1992, and he was back in 1994 and 1995 to share Christmas with us at the new house. In other words, golf has brought everyone together in a way which might never have happened without it.

At the same time as Tony was developing the management side of my affairs, my mother took on something of an accountancy role. When I am flying back from a six-week spell in the States, I will put receipts from each week in separate envelopes for her to sort out.

She is the first to notice if I am wasting money and, though I don't like to admit it, I do take a bit of notice. If, for instance, I am heading for a night at my gambling club at the Ritz, she will voice her displeasure at the outset. I will go just the same, but her comments stay with me and definitely have some sort of a restraining influence. If she were to say, 'On you go, dear, and enjoy yourself!' I'd probably go wild.

Chapter 4

The Natural Athlete

It was on the way back from my win in the US Open in 1987 that someone asked – and they could not have done it more nicely – if I minded being big. My reply was not entirely to the point, but it was the truth. I explained that when the rest of the professionals watched highlights of the golf on television, the kind of thing they noticed was the angle of their clubhead at the top of the back-swing. In contrast, the only thing I wanted to see was whether my shoulders looked huge.

I was similarly self-conscious out on the course, taking every chance to dart behind leaderboards and trees if I thought the television cameras were focusing on me.

In those days, people used to ask why I wore a tank top or a sweater even on the hottest days. I would reply, glibly, that I hadn't noticed that it was particularly hot. The truth was that I was absolutely baking. It was simply my impression that I looked less big if I wore something which covered me up a bit.

A lot of my friends did their best to make me feel good about my size, and I remember learning of a particularly reassuring comment from Barb Thomas, a member of the LPGA staff. 'For a large girl,' Barb once said to the American press, 'Laura looks really good. She could definitely teach some of our fuller-figured professionals a thing or two.'

Others would tell me that I had big bones and that I was never meant to be slim. In fact, the only person who had the courage to say anything adverse was Gary Player. He saw me drinking Coca-Colas at a Ford pro-am in France and asked me how many of them I had in a day. When I confessed that it could be anything up to 15, I almost caused this extraordinarily fit little golfer to collapse. He told me I was in danger of becoming a 'Coca-holic' and made me promise to cut down because of the ridiculously high sugar intake.

I never allowed myself to dwell long and hard on how I needed to go on a diet. Instead, the idea was suddenly detonated by a television advert I saw for Ultra-Slim-Fast, then the American version of our own Slim-Fast drinks. The man promoting the product was Tommy Lasorda from the Los Angeles Dodgers. I had remembered him as a truly massive Italian, yet here he was on the screen looking trim and fit and telling people that anyone could pick up Ultra-Slim-Fast in their local supermarket.

Those who know me best would appreciate that I am not the kind of person to go up to a chemist's counter and ask for a slimming drink. That would embarrass me no end. It was the fact that you could fling a packet into an anonymous supermarket trolley which made all the difference. I picked out a packet of chocolate-flavoured sachets and, back in my motel room, made myself up a glass before I set off for the golf course.

I shot a 62 that day and, superstitious soul that I am, I at once linked the good round to the slimming drink. I had good vibes about it.

By the time of the Longines Classic in October 1992, I had shed a couple of stone and the press had cottoned on to what they called my disappearing act. I admitted that I was on a diet and, before too long, I had an offer from the *Sun* newspaper to slim along with them, whatever that was supposed to mean. Not fancying any regular, public weigh-ins, I declined. Yet I have to say that the interest everyone was showing definitely helped.

Particularly in America, the club playing host, together with other clubs in the area, will provide volunteer marshals at a tournament. These are wonderful people and you are apt to see them on the same hole and in the same position year after year. They become familiar faces and, as I lost weight, it was lovely to have them greeting me with a gasp before saying something complimentary about my new figure.

My target weight was 13 stone and, by the Nabisco Dinah Shore event of April 1993, the new Laura, so to speak, was really beginning to take shape. Where once I used to grab a Mars Bar if I felt hungry on the course, I was now tucking into an apple or a banana. (To be honest, I don't really like to be seen eating when I'm playing. There's always some so-and-so with a camera who will catch you at it and all you are doing is feeding the papers with a story.)

By June 1992, I had lost three and a half stone and was down to my target weight. Thirteen stone was about right; I was never going to be a ballerina. Then – and this is so typical of me – I began to get bored with it all.

What further served to slacken my resolve was a chance remark from Florence Descampe. She said to me that her doctor had told her that I should stop dieting for a while. He said I was looking a bit run down. (I myself don't go near doctors, so that was as close to a medical opinion as I was going to get.)

Also my golf was not that brilliant at the time. My swing had not suffered, but my concentration was not at its best. I cannot put my hand on my heart and say that that was definitely down to the slimming. It might have been no more than a coincidence, but the mere possibility made it a little easier for me to convince myself that I was making a wise decision in stopping the Slim-Fast.

Of the three and a half stone I took off, I have put back one and three-quarters and have remained steady at that. I deserve at least some marks, because the lifestyle is not the most helpful if, like me, you are constantly having to watch your weight.

Life revolves around my tee-off time and dinner. If I have an early tee-off time, I do not bother with breakfast. (Despite what the experts are supposed to say, it doesn't seem to do me any harm to play on an empty stomach.) If, on the other hand, I have a later tee-off time, I will have a good early morning meal.

I have stopped eating chocolate and bags of crisps during the day, and Gary Player would be pleased to learn that I have never gone back to my habit of knocking back the Coca-Colas. I now have three or four diet drinks per day, but no more. I look forward to my dinner and enjoy it, though I don't go mad. For instance, I am nowadays more likely to order a baked potato than chips.

In conjunction with these improved eating habits, I will go running round the perimeter of the garden if I have had a couple of weeks off and need to build up my fitness. That seems to work, while it obviously does no harm that I am always playing other games. I get a lot of use out of my football pitch and tennis court at home and have endless games of cricket and football when I am on tour. The American professionals think it more than passing strange, but the caddies and the other British players are always keen to get involved.

This year, I was finally persuaded to go to the mobile gym with my friends. I was working out on the bike and even going so far as to join the rest for aerobics. The reason I have not put this in the present tense is that I cannot promise that I will still be doing it when this book appears. In March, I placed a £50 bet with Helen Dobson that I would keep it up for at least a month, and the chances are that I might just have seen the scooping up of that little sum as the end of the exercise.

People have suggested that I cannot be fit because I am so big, but that is not the case. Confirmation came from the fitness trainer on the LPGA tour. He had been telling one of the press that I had never been into the fitness trailer other than to ask for a bandage, and went on to say that I was one of the most natural athletes he had ever known.

To sum up, I'm not at all sure I'd prefer to be smaller but shorter off the tee. I am as I am, and, as I like to remind myself, life has dealt me a wonderful hand.

Chapter 5

Imitation, the Name of the Game

I hope it will reassure you when I say that my opinions on how best to get started in golf have never altered. As I said in my first book, *Carefree Golf*, eight years ago, if someone were to give me a ten-year-old boy to teach, I would buy him a video of his favourite player before telling him to copy what he saw.

I am not against coaching, but I do firmly believe that there can be an alternative. Lessons are obviously of great value to some, but it is my conviction that they must be combined with long periods on the practice ground. The pupil must do more than simply repeat what the professional has advised. Only by experimenting with every kind of shot can a golfer really be at one with his or her clubs.

Dave Regan, the professional at West Byfleet, where I played most of my amateur golf, advised early on that the best lesson he could give me was 'not to take lessons'. But he only said as much after he had satisfied himself that I was going about my golfing business in a way which was right for me.

Nick Price, as I see it, approaches his lesson-taking in exactly the right manner. When, for example, someone was asking how contrasting characters such as he and Nick Faldo could each see David Leadbetter as the ideal teacher, Price explained that the two of them asked very different questions of the guru.

'Nick,' said Price, of Faldo, 'prefers to have David standing over him the whole time. For myself, if I'm with David for three hours, I will have enough material to keep me happy for six weeks. I like to interpret what he has said and gradually, little by little, incorporate it into my game.

'On the same tack,' he continued, 'I like to go out and hit balls without David's scrutiny. If he were watching me all the time, I'd end up wrapping my driver round his neck. Either that, or I'd become hopelessly dependent on him.'

When I was on *Sport in Question* shortly before the 1995 Masters, I was asked about Nick Faldo and I dared to suggest that he would benefit enormously from giving more rein to the natural golfer within him. However, I do believe that there is one area where Faldo's degree of precision is vital. Namely, the set-up. To me, alignment matters more than anything else. If a player's alignment isn't good, he or she is never going to hit fairways or greens. (See section on driving.)

When it comes to the grip, I do not feel quite so strongly, largely because people have often advised that my hold on the club is too strong. What you have to find is a grip which works well with your swing. If what the experts describe as the perfect grip does not feel comfortable after a reasonably extended trial, don't use it.

Were you to press me further, I would opt for an amalgam of what is comfortable and what is correct. Mine is a strongish version of the Vardon or overlapping grip, though people always seem to be fascinated when I tell them that I had a two-handed grip throughout my amateur career.*

---

* The truth is that Laura can, within reason, play with any grip. She duly demonstrated that versatility in the South of France in the Longines Classic of 1991.

That day, having sliced the top from the index finger of her left hand, she switched to an interlocking grip and promptly went out and shot a 66, which took in her first hole-in-one in 14 years in golf. As one who savoured the good things in life, the late Sir Henry Cotton would have approved the way in which she had decapitated that digit – namely, in opening a tin of caviare.

Incidentally, I no longer move my hands up and down the shaft as I did in the days when I won my British and US Opens. In May 1988, Phil Tresidder wrote in *Golf Digest*: 'Laura's grip is startling to the connoisseur, with some six inches or more at the top of the stick clearly visible while her hands choke down so that the bottom fingers are almost on the metal. The driver seems a mere match-stick in her hands.'

The habit dates from my second year on tour, when I was looking for a bit of extra control with the long irons. From there it crept into all my other shots, the positioning becoming something of a comfort zone I sought in times of pressure.

Dave Marr, in commenting on my US Open win, was bemused rather than critical, and suggested that if Ray Floyd could get away with that particular idiosyncrasy, so could I. Again, he noted that if it was costing me a few yards, that did not matter over much. Not, he said, when I was thumping my drives comfortably past the 270-yard mark.

In *Carefree Golf*, I suggested that this precautionary gripping down the shaft was probably no more than a passing fad. And in saying as much, I cited what Lee Trevino once said to Nancy Lopez: 'For as long as your swing works, keep it as it is. The time to change is when it stops working.' I stopped the 'down-the-shaft' tendency in the summer of 1993, almost without knowing it. Today, my hands alight on the same stretch of grip every time.

I cannot emphasize too strongly that my swing does not operate on a series of potted instructions but on the overall pictures I have in my mind; pictures which have been built up and constantly refurbished through years of following golf on television and visiting major tournaments. On several occasions, for example, I have been to the Masters at Augusta. Once there, I don't just swan around and buy mementoes. All the time, I try to get into a position where I can really see the top players and soak up some of their talent. This is what I wrote on the subject in *Carefree Golf*:

'When I look at top players such as Bernhard Langer and Seve Ballesteros, I am trying, first and foremost, to pick up their rhythm. Having watched them hit a few shots, I play those shots over and over again in my head, almost as I would a song. Then, when I go to the practice ground, all I am trying to do is to reproduce that timing and feel.'

Since my belief in imitation is so strong, I have devoted the next section of the book to suggesting what it is the reader should look for in the way the better players go about their golf and what they might usefully borrow from their swings. I am hoping readers will see it as a helpful reference guide when watching the game on television.

Amy Alcott

Feeling your Way Round

Amy's golf is very much her own. She's a bit of a Lee Trevino in the way she will shape her shots this way and that – nudging the ball one minute, punching it the next. An extraordinary shotmaker who you would think had been brought up on a British links rather than in America, Amy has an answer for everything. I would never recommend anyone to copy the way she sets about every shot so differently, but she is definitely one to study on the matter of course management. When you watch her, you find yourself asking, 'Why is she doing this . . . why is she doing that?' A round with Amy makes me appreciate my own shortcomings in this area.

Amy's 'One, Two, Three' drill has often been extremely useful to those struggling with rhythm: 'On "One",' as she writes in *Amy Alcott's Guide to Women's Golf*, 'I make my forward press and begin my backswing. "Two" takes me to the top of my swing, and on "Three" I'm making contact.' Amy herself will often count aloud while practising.

Helen Alfresson

Striking the Right Note

Watching Helen play, you would want some of her competitiveness to rub off on you, but not all of it. She is possibly the fiercest competitor I have ever met. On her day, there is no one better, but you can see in Helen the dangers of being just too intense, of having expectations which are too high. I used to break into a canter when I had a bad hole, and there were times when it gave me the feeling that I was leaving trouble behind. However, I long ago realized that the best long-term solution – and it probably applies to everyone – is to stay calm, and to try and bring a more equable temperament to bear.

Seve Ballesteros

A Natural Improvises

A natural rather than a made golfer, Seve has always seen the swing predominantly in terms of his right side, arm and hand. He may hit more than his share of wayward shots, but he also hits far more of what the tennis fraternity would call outright winners.

Having played so much of his boyhood golf armed only with a three iron, he knows how to improvise – and never more so than when he is in the vicinity of the green. Watch him to bring new life to a tired short game.

As Ben Crenshaw says of Seve, no one sees more clearly the shot that has to be played; no one has more imagination.

Pat Bradley

In the Eye of the Beholder

I am sure that a lot of people take one look at Pat Bradley's swing and think to themselves, 'She's a bit out of her depth.' Yet she is arguably the most professional of all the pros in the way she gets her job done. The swing does not look good, nor does she hit a lot of perfect shots. But she gets the ball in the hole and has done it often enough to have won a place in the LPGA's Hall of Fame. Too many golfers dream of being Nick Faldo and hitting every shot bang out of the middle. Some of them would get far better results were they to make a study of Pat Bradley grinding out the figures.

Pat lost her game a few years ago when, though she did not know it at the time, she had a thyroid condition. She fell from 15th to 109th on the money list and, after missing yet another cut, would leave her hotel in the small hours of the morning in order to avoid having to talk to the press.

Once she had been correctly diagnosed, there was no stopping her. From 109th in 1988, she rose to fourth in 1989. All her sister professionals were thrilled for her in 1991 when, three years after the illness which seemed to be spelling the end of her career, she finished first on the money list and was admitted to the Hall of Fame.

JoAnne Carner

A Switch of Emphasis

What an incredible champion she is! JoAnne is in her middle fifties, but I am prepared to bet good money that she will win again on the LPGA tour. She does not fight the fact that she has lost a lot of the length for which she was famed. Instead, she has worked overtime on her short game, and the results are breathtaking. Watch her bunker play and it will give you a new insight into the possibilities from sand.

JoAnne captained the Americans in the Solheim Cup at The Greenbrier and her own old relish for match-play fired up her entire team.

John Daly

Looking Beyond the Long Shots

Everyone goes to watch John Daly to see how far he hits. I know myself that there is nothing to match the experience of standing beside him on the tee when he gives one of his mammoth drives the full treatment. These are shots which, to adapt a famous David Feherty quip, demand that he include the curvature of the earth in his calculations. However, it is a mistake to be carried away with his long game to the point where you don't notice what he can do on and around the green. His touch is magic – and that, as Jack Nicklaus says, is why John Daly has won two majors.

Beth Daniel

Thriving On Five-Footers

For a picture-perfect swing, Beth Daniel's is the answer. Her short game is nothing special, but her management of the five-footer is possibly the best in the women's game. I would say she makes nine out of ten of this length and that is why she has won so often on tour.

Ernie Els

The Champion's Champion

That Nick Faldo watches Ernie Els's swing should surely be a good enough recommendation for the rest of us. To my way of thinking, Ernie's rhythm is something which comes from within. I think it was Greg Norman who said that the South African was born with the kind of level-headed approach which Norman himself had taken fifteen years to master.

Nick Faldo

Stick or Twist

A unique player, as close to a machine as you can get. He is among those who respond well to a lot of technical analysis, but I am not convinced that there are all that many in that mould. I have known players make themselves permanently worse rather than better through making changes. As a professional, your lifespan is relatively short and, if you make major alterations, your confidence can take a terrible knock in the process. Ian Woosnam would seem to bear out what I am saying. He went through the business of changing an awful lot of things before deciding that he was better off with what he had got.

At the time of writing, I have my fingers crossed for Helen Dobson, the brilliantly gifted former English and British champion who started going to Mitchell Spearman, one of Leadbetter's men, at the end of 1994. She has altered absolutely everything, and I'm just hoping that she will get it all together again. Changing a working swing is a big decision and not one which anyone should take lightly.

Going back to Faldo himself, he knows that rhythm is not something that can be plucked from the textbook. During the 1995 Nedbank Million Dollar tournament at Sun City, he was saying that the reason he was so pleased to partner Ernie Els in the first round was because he likes to watch the South African's tempo.

Jane Geddes

A New Day Dawns

There is an excellent lesson to be learnt from Jane Geddes. She is what I call a streak player. She can do a 79 one day and then, for no apparent reason, hand in a 63 the next. Yet there is a reason. Where many of us, after a poor opening round, are thinking in the back of our minds that this simply isn't our week, Jane manages to shrug off all negative thoughts and start afresh. That approach works for her time and time again – I know, because I've been there when it has happened.

Trish Johnson

Escaping the Comfort Zone

Most of us have what I call a comfort zone. For myself, I had two legitimate chances to break 60 and blew them both. A small voice inside was telling me I couldn't do it. The occasion which hurt the more was in Toledo in 1991, where I needed to finish birdie, eagle, birdie, or par, eagle, eagle. The latter option was perfectly possible in that the course finishes with two par fives. Instead, I finished 6,5,6 for what was arguably the most disappointing 66 of my life.

Trish is not the world's greatest striker, but she has what it takes to keep attacking, never to get scared. If she has made seven birdies in a row, she is thinking of an eighth.

I've seen high-handicap players with this gift, too; for example a 25 handicapper who, on his day, does not take fright at the idea of handing in a card to 12. To a large extent, it's God-given, but we can all work on stretching the comfort zone.

It will be interesting to see how Rebecca Hudson, the top English girl golfer at the time of writing, turns out in the next few years. In the summer of 1995, when she was 16, Rebecca handed in a ten-under-par 63 at Wheatley in the Danum Cup. Some will describe the round as a fluke, but I would disagree. A hole-in-one is what I call a fluke. When you put together a low score over 18 holes, you are being tested in all directions. It has to augur well for Rebecca that she had the mental control to pin down the good figures and to keep that good run going.

Betsy King

Giving Nothing Away

Betsy is the ultimate in terms of giving nothing away. To look at her, you would not have a clue as to whether she was five under par or five over. It is a virtue which works well for her on the LPGA tour but one which is still more important in match-play. You never want to let an opponent know that you are feeling ruffled at having lost a hole. Do that, and she will tee up at the next with a double dose of confidence.

Bernhard Langer

Mental Strength

I have the greatest admiration for Bernhard Langer. He has to be the patron saint for all those who feel that they are never going to master this game. One attack of the yips is enough to ruin most golfers, but Bernhard has come back from three such attacks.

There were times when people would gloat at the side of the practice putting green as he stood there trying to find a cure, but he was never going to accept that his twitch was terminal. He always contrived to keep his problem in perspective.

Aside from drawing inspiration from the number of putts he holes today, everyone should watch Bernhard's easy mastery of the middle and longer irons.

Bernhard talks a lot about keeping the spine angle constant. In simple terms, he means neither jumping up nor dipping down in mid-swing, which makes a lot of sense.

Nancy Lopez

Keeping the Bogey at Bay
If Nancy is in the trees off the tee, her thought process is different from that of almost all of her sister professionals. For a start, there is no sign of any anger, nor does she unsettle herself – as I tend to do – by letting her imagination run riot as she dreams up some dramatic recovery. Instead, she will play an unspectacular shot out of the trouble before coming up with a mind-bogglingly brilliant iron to the green.

Ninety per cent of the time, she will save her par. If I were asked to recommend how a party of aspiring young golfers should spend an afternoon at an LPGA tournament, I would definitely want them to see that aspect of Nancy's game. It is a lesson which would probably save them a lot of shots and a lot of money over the years.

Phil Mickelson

Getting it Right the Wrong Way Round
If you are left-handed, it is a mistake to try to translate the right-handed technique you read about into a left-handed one. The golf swing is a difficult enough business at the best of times without making it more so. If I were a left-hander I would take every possible opportunity to watch a player such as Phil Mickelson. Phil, who is actually right-handed in everything but golf, has a handsome swing and a lovely rhythm.

His confidence over the medium-length pitch is such that he gives it a big, full swing rather than a controlled punch.

Left-handed golfers are further blessed in having one of the best putters in the world in their ranks in Bob Charles. Charles, of course, won our Open in 1963 and, to watch him, you will need to tune into the senior tour.

A little diversion . . . I learnt, recently, of an elderly Indian couple who play at the Delhi Golf Club. Years ago, they underwent an arranged marriage and, three months into married life, they set out for their first game of golf. To their mingled amazement and delight, they discovered that they were both left-handed. Presumably, if they needed any confirmation that their parents had made the right choice for them, that was it.

Colin Montgomerie

The Full Monty

Colin, to my mind, is a prime example of a player who did not go berserk when he turned professional and instead stuck with the full, flowing swing which had served him so well in his amateur career. What has always surprised me about Colin is that however hot and bothered he gets with things going on around him, it rarely shows in his swing.

He maintains the same easy rhythm all the time, and that is why he has succeeded in winning the Volvo Order of Merit three times in a row.

Lotta Neumann

Tempo

Lotta is tempo personified and, in that respect, she is probably the women's equivalent of Ernie Els. I like playing with her, because watching her swing can have a soothing effect on your own. Her fairway woods are out on their own; she's one of the few people who make them look easy as she sweeps them off the turf with the minimum of fuss. As I mention in the section on woods, she has a seven which is tantamount to a magic wand, and now she has what they call a 'divine nine'. She says the nine wood is the equivalent of her five iron.

Alison Nicholas

A Five-Footer to Fear

Alison refers to herself as being 'five feet in my studs'. Too small for the tennis she loved in teenage days, Alison nowadays works as no one else on the women's tour. She has developed her technique under Lawrence Farmer and, at the same time, built up the kind of muscles needed to make the best of her new, flatter swing. Paul Darby, the fitness expert, has helped her in that department, and she will tell you that this two-pronged approach has not only given her some extra length but made her more confident with the longer irons.

Ali has been a great partner to me in the Solheim Cup. Time and time again, our games have clicked perfectly. We bring out the best in each other and work as a team all the time. If, for instance, one of us starts off playing better than other, the relationship doesn't suffer. We want the best for each other all the time, and that even applies when we are playing as individuals in a tournament. When Ali beat me by a shot to win the 1987 British Women's Open at St Mellion, I remember saying to her that if someone had to beat me, there was no one I would rather have do it.

I have always thought of Ali as the best long putter in the business but, in the last year or so, she has also become very strong on the shorter ones. Her determination is nothing short of phenomenal.

Jack Nicklaus

Looking at the Whole

When I played with Jack Nicklaus at the end of 1995, I saw first hand what I already knew about his ability to graft. He himself says that he has never been too proud to admit that several of his majors were more the result of others losing than him winning. He calls it his 'one-shot-at-a-time, keep cool, golf's an 18-hole game attitude'. He never fails to make the best of a difficult situation, reaping much the same confidence from any smart bit of recovery work as he might from notching an eagle. That's what being a good competitor is all about.

Another thing that struck me about Jack Nicklaus when we played at Muirfield Village was the attention he gave to his opening drive. This is something which I have always done myself, though, to my still lingering irritation, I did not get a good one away when I played with him. In his book, *Playing Lessons*, Jack picked out the first shot as the most important in a round: 'Hit it well and confidence surges. Hit it poorly and sour thoughts immediately begin to flood the psyche. They may go away if you play the next shot well, but too often you won't because doubt has already been planted. So try your darndest for a strong opener.'

Where I try above all to have a good picture in my mind of my opening shot, Jack Nicklaus says that his key is to concentrate on being deliberate. That, for him, counters 'an involuntary urge to hurry the shot and shorten the agony'. He likes to have a few deep breaths as he walks on to the tee, along with a few slow and easy practice swings.

Dottie Pepper

Her Way

I wouldn't want to play the way Dottie plays, but it certainly works for her. She is glaringly intense. She shouts and yells at the ball and her game is fuelled by that anger. JoAnne Carner, America's Solheim Cup captain at the last time of asking, gave the Dottie Pepper method her approval at The Greenbrier when she said that she preferred to see a player getting mad rather than doing a Ben Hogan and showing no emotion at all. Myself, I would never recommend it.

Nick Price

A Certain Sameness

I have never played with Nick Price, but what strikes me most is the consistency of his swing with everything from a driver through to a sand iron. His tempo is fast, but the swing is always the same. (He will tell you he has altered it a bit in the last year, swinging back on a flatter plane which is more in keeping with his downswing.)

The message we can all take from Nick is that if you can bring the same swing to bear every time, your chances of being a consistent golfer are that much better than if you are all the time tinkering with your action.

Another interesting point about the Zimbabwean concerns the way in which he traced his loss of form in 1995 to the fact that he had become too caught up in all the commitments resulting from 1994, his Open championship year. He said he never had a moment to himself. He dealt with this by setting up an office away from his home and installing a couple of girls to take on the work which had been so getting him down. A matter of clearing the decks in order to be able to give the game, and his family, his best shot.

Patty Sheehan

Making Your Own Luck

Patty is one of those players who make their own luck. It's not always easy to do, but it certainly isn't born of making negative comments and expecting the worst all the time. Unlike Patty, I used to be very guilty of that myself. These days, you will never hear me being negative, making excuses. It took me a long time to get out of that self-destruct cycle, but now, whatever the situation, I'll find a positive side and tell myself that things are going to be all right. If, for instance, I'm having a bad day on the greens, I think less about the ones I have missed than the fact that the putts ahead are bound to start dropping at some point. It may be worth mentioning that I no longer switch putters as much as I did in my more negative days. My thinking, then, was that each of them in turn deserved to be dropped. That was another manifestation of the old saw about a bad workman . . .

Annika Sorenstam

Head Up
It is very much a Swedish thing. Annika loses her rag but always gets her act back together before the next shot. She's a great player, and you can forget what people say about her habit of having her head up as she hits through the ball. It works for her because she has such an incredible feel for the game. I don't doubt that if someone were too tell her to concentrate on keeping her head firmly in place, she would lose something of her natural feel and flow. Mark you, she has been working on staying down fractionally longer without any ill effect.

In the first draft for this book, I suggested that Annika would win at any moment, and that was precisely what happened. She won twice in Europe before going on to capture the US Women's Open. She finished at the top of both the 1995 American money list and our own. I have to admit that it hurt that she should beat me into second place in both, but I had to hand it to her. For months, she hit one perfect shot after another and she continued to do as much this year, winning her second US Open. Some feat.

Sam Torrance

A Lasting Love of Golf
Sam takes unhurried puffs on his cigarette and swings in the same easy vein. He's like another Scot, Dale Reid, in the way in which you can seldom tell from his demeanour whether he has hit a good shot or the reverse. He has been beautifully taught by his father, but, to me, the best thing about Sam is that, though the game is very much his life, he does know how to relax.

Like Colin Montgomerie, to whom he lost on the 1995 Volvo European Tour, Sam likes the odd drink and he enjoys his food. Equally, I doubt whether Sam spends too much time jogging or working out in the gym. He keeps the fun in his professional career and that is why he, like me, can handle a tightly packed schedule.

On the subject of Sam's broomhandle putter, he's absolutely right to use whatever works for him. Myself, I wouldn't be seen dead with one, but that, of course, is just me.

Karrie Webb

Down Under to Up Top
Karrie, as I write, is having an amazing rookie year in America. Having won the Weetabix British Open, she qualified for the Tournament of Champions at the start of 1996 and went on to finish second. Then, the following week, she had a win to set alongside her British Open triumph.

The easiest way to describe the Australian is to say that she is like another Annika Sorenstam, but with a little extra length. Her swing is simple and always the same. Like a catchy tune, hers is a very easy rhythm to superimpose on your own swing.

Ian Woosnam

A Career Regenerated
What a shotmaker! His long irons, coupled with his ability to manufacture a shot for every circumstance, are out of this world. I was not a bit surprised at the way he started the 1996 season; he might have been erratic in 1995, but his shots still had a simmering brilliance about them. They were never those of a player who had lost it.

I am definitely a better golfer through having played alongside him. In fact, I felt like his apprentice as I tried to take on board all the little shots he produced around the greens.

Ian taught himself and the rest of us a good lesson at last year's Volvo German Masters. He was struggling with his putting at the time and, in his second round, he went out with both his normal putter and a Torrance-type broomhandle putter in his bag. He started bringing out the broomhandle model on the 12th green and, thereafter, he was at a loss to know which implement he should employ.

The next day, the broomhandle putter was absent. As he said himself, it had to be one or the other.

Chapter 6

The Tools for the Job

WOODS

I carry a driver and a three wood, but that is not to say that you should do the same. The reason I have only a couple of woods in my bags is that I am happier than most with my longer irons. I did try a seven wood at a time when the more lofted woods were very much on the way in, but I knocked it as high as I knocked it far. It gave the wind too much of a say.

Several of my friends are dab hands with these clubs. Like Annika Sorenstam, Lotta Neumann carries a nine wood, and in any contest between me with my five iron and Lotta with her nine wood, she would win every time. In the men's world, Lee Trevino is a magician with his seven wood, while you might be surprised to learn that Sam Torrance is a great seven-wood man. He dropped his two iron a couple of years ago on the grounds that he hits the ball so low and far with a three iron that he doesn't need to resort to a two.

There is a 540-yard par five at Sun City, admittedly downhill, which he hit with his drive and seven wood in the second round of last year's Million Dollar tournament. The club enabled him to get the height he needed to fly the water and stop his ball about ten feet from the hole on his way to an eagle. Most of the world's top players were hitting long irons which took a couple of bounces before ending up in the barbed wire-like semi-rough at the back.

When Sam was asked about his seven wood he replied, 'It may

be an old man's club, but it's made me a fortune.' As is the case with his broomhandle putter, he doesn't mind what people think if the club is right for him.

Nick Price is another who likes the feel of the higher woods. Though he does not carry one all the time, he will tell you that he always has a four or five wood at the ready for Augusta. Ray Floyd, when he won the Masters in 1976, said that his five wood had been his 'key' club.

For some reason or another, the level of expectation the professionals acquire with these implements is quite extraordinary.

I have known handicap ladies, too, who have an uncanny affinity with their higher woods. They should not let anyone talk them into believing that the these clubs are a soft option. Remember, you don't get any extra marks for using the longer irons. Like Torrance, you must simply make up your mind to go with the clubs which work best for you.

I fell out with my driver for a full season in 1991, and in winning the Inamori Classic on the LPGA tour I used my two iron all the way. I don't think the Americans could quite believe it. However, the trial separation did no lasting damage. Today I use my driver – a Maruman model – with all the relish I did in teenage days.

When I look at any of the photographic sequences of my drive, I am apt to think of all the things which will have gone before that moment when I am ready to take the club away. To start with, I will normally have teed up so the top of the ball is about a quarter of an inch above the clubhead. When I am going for a really big drive, I might tee it a little higher.

In contrast, when I am looking for accuracy above all else, I will often hit the ball off the deck, not bothering with a tee peg at all. That is how I hit from the 17th tee *en route* to winning the 1995 English Open at The Oxfordshire. I needed a long, straight tee shot and that is precisely what I got. It enabled me to carry the gaping water with my two iron while others were happy enough to play short of the lake in two and catch the green in three. (Before anyone reminds me, I will admit that I wasted my efforts some-what by taking three putts. However, hitting the perfect tee shot under such pressure was a boost in itself.)

I have always paid a lot of attention to my set-up, especially since that time a few years ago when I realized that I had this tendency to open my stance further and further when everything was going well. It was linked to an irrepressible urge to hit harder and harder.

I have never found any better method for lining up than the old tram-line routine of picking a spot a foot or so in front of the ball and then placing the feet on the line running parallel to that one. The position of the ball will be just inside my left foot.

You cannot afford to be of no fixed address, so to speak. Setting up correctly every time is arguably the most important thing you have to do. Ask Fanny Sunesson, who caddies for Nick Faldo. In all her years of caddying for Nick, she says that his attention to detail here is the thing which has rubbed off the most on her golf. If your alignment is awry, not even the best swing in the world is going to save you.

I have to say that I was greatly taken with a suggestion in Harvey Penick's *Little Blue Golf Book* for women. Penick told how one of his old pupils, Shelly Mayfield, had found the perfect way of checking up on his stance. During a period in which he was hitting the ball especially well, he had got this big piece of cardboard and drawn on it the position of his feet and that of the ball.

After that, if ever Mayfield started pushing or pulling, he was able to haul out the piece of cardboard and check that everything was in order. I am lucky in that Matthew is able to keep a constant check on my alignment, but, for the golfer who has no one to keep an eye on it, the cardboard template sounds an excellent solution. Better by far than asking the opinion of different friends who are not entirely sure what they are looking for.

By way of convincing myself that all is well before I hit, I will look up several times to see where I am going and commit the relevant landing area to memory. I do not take aim on any tiny target. Instead, I see a stretch the width of a goalmouth and try to imagine the ball finishing up in the middle.

This picture of where you are bound is vital. Too many women golfers are just preoccupied with trying to manipulate or steer the ball somewhere down the fairway; too many men launch themselves at the ball with no aim in mind beyond belting the ball past a playing companion. Male pro-am partners, as I have said elsewhere, try to do this to me all the time. Maybe they will outdrive me once or twice, but the chances are that they will lose their timing and generally have a bad driving day.

As you know, I am not one for breaking the swing down to a series of instructions. In fact, when I read what the 'experts' say about my swing, I find it difficult to take in that they are talking about me. To my mind, nothing is more calculated to interfere with the flow of the swing than dissecting it. If the set-up and the alignment are correct, it's my belief that you are perfectly placed to imitate one of the many good swings you will see on your television. After all, if you wanted to learn a new song, you would do much better to listen to it than to be told that you needed to hop from C sharp to B flat, to E and to F, or whatever.

All I would say, when looking at my swing sequence on these pages, is that the action looks compact but that it is easy to detect the slight sway which has been with me all my days. Some people pick on it as a fault but, though I did overdo it in 1990, I am under the impression that much of my power comes from the movement. (Note how I keep my right knee tucked in a bit, because if that joint gives way, the power will disappear.) I know that players like John Daly and Colin Montgomerie thrive on a full, flowing swing, but I have always preferred a shorter version, the reason being that there is so much less to go wrong.

If you look at any picture of me at the top of the swing, the power almost shows. At that point, I am still looking at the back of the ball and am not conscious of any kind of pause before the downswing. Instead, I have this feeling of the swing being one flowing movement.

I keep my head down as I accelerate through the ball, and my follow-through is long without being loose. What you are looking for is what I would call controlled aggression as opposed to an absolute thrash.

At the swing's end, you should be well balanced. Someone in my gallery was saying not too long ago that they never bothered to watch where my ball landed. They simply watched me. They knew that if I was holding my follow-through the shot had been a good one. Look at Torrance, and you can tell if he has got a good one away by the manner in which he moves straight from a good finish to pick up his tee peg. He will have glanced up to check that the ball is sailing down the middle but he does not follow its flight like the crowds follow it.

The average man and the average woman are at the opposite ends of the spectrum in terms of what they put into the hit. As I have already suggested, women tend to be over-cautious, whereas men will go hell for leather at the ball.

I have always felt that women golfers have what it takes to hit the ball farther than they do, my oft-repeated view being that it has something to do with husbands constantly advising their wives to put down an old ball in case they should top it into the water. In other words, I think of the problem as more mental than physical. Whatever the reason, it is a pity, because these women I have in mind are often beautifully schooled in terms of set-up and take-away. All the trouble stems from a deceleration on the down-swing.

What I am saying is not too far removed from what Harvey Penick wrote in a passage entitled 'Hit it Hard'. He told of this woman whose practice swings were lovely – slow and rhythmic. He stuck a tee peg in the ground and asked her to hit the ball using precisely the same sweet swing. 'She used her sweet swing and hit the tee and never even bent it sideways before she finished in a well-balanced follow-through.'

He exhorted her to hit it again, with the words, 'Hit it hard, this time.'

The same swing followed and, said Penick, 'her clubface hit the ground and didn't bounce, much less cut a divot.'

Penick's verdict was that she cared more about looking good than 'swatting her ball down the fairway'. He sent her away to swing a weighted club every day, something which would automatically help her to develop a bit of golfing muscle.

The woman golfer who is not physically strong is going to need to build herself up if she is to come up with the kind of hit I have in mind. I know I have a lot of natural strength, but I can guarantee that at least some of my length stems from the other sports I play and have always played. If two women were to stand up at a driving range by way of a first golf outing, with one of them having played regular games of tennis and the other having taken no such exercise, there is no question that the tennis player would hit the longer golf ball.

Swimming is another useful sport for developing the kind of solid strength which will serve the golfer well. Christine Trew, Sandy Lyle's first wife, was a swimmer-turned-golfer and she always gave the ball a healthy whack.

Another course of action the soft hitter could take is to listen to the crash of ball on clubhead produced by a hard-hitting man – for, whatever their other faults, most men have it in them to give the ball an uninhibited belt.

Another point I would make is that you must move with the times in terms of equipment, just as you would alter what you wear to accommodate the latest fashions. Sticking with the same old persimmon driver will pay off only for a small minority. The technology is there and you must use it. How many tennis players do you still see using a small-headed, wooden racket?

The bigger-headed drivers have given many a player a new lease of life. They have a larger sweet spot and this, in turn, will lead to a bigger percentage of drives reacting as if they were hit bang out of the middle. It is not just the manufacturers who make those extraordinary claims about new drivers which will add an extra 20 or 30 yards. The professionals talk along precisely the same lines. Gary Player, for instance, was noticing a marked loss of length in 1995 before he designed himself a new driver which gave him a further 30 yards. After that, he said he was back hitting par fives which he hadn't reached in two in years. All right, he has a vested interest, but even so . . .

Nick Price, by all accounts, was positively ecstatic towards the end of last year because he had helped with the design of a one-piece club with a graphite shaft and steel head bonded together. It was difficult for someone like myself, who is more interested in the end result than what goes into the club, to get to grips with it all, but he talked of an 11-degree driver which will be the making of the higher-handicap golfers. He said it will look like a three wood but, because of the higher centre of gravity, it will not send the ball soaring. To recap, you must try to keep pace with the latest developments because, if you don't, your opponent will.

Shaping the Ball

Getting a touch of draw or fade on the ball could not be more simple. If you want to draw the ball a shade, take up your usual stance and have the clubface square before moving the right foot back a couple of inches. Allow your right shoulder to move back in keeping with the foot. Simply by adjusting your position at the address you will swing back on the inside and your eventual angle of attack will be such as to impart a hook. The reverse applies for a fade. Open your stance, open your shoulders. You will then be poised to swing back outside the line. It is simple, and you should never allow anyone to tell you otherwise.

As with all others, these shots require practice. A few carefully executed draws and fades under the eye of your professional are not enough. Use the practice ground to have fun experimenting with the different shapes of shot.

A long Way

Not too long ago, Nancy Lopez was joking that she hated playing alongside me because I hit the ball 'a million miles'. Hitting a long ball is by no means everything, but there are huge advantages. As Nancy says, it is a bit daunting to be constantly outdriven; I had a dose of my own medicine when I played with John Daly and Jack Nicklaus a later in the Wendy's Three-Tour Challenge. As I explain in a later chapter, John, with his immense wind-up and that long swing to go with it, was thrashing the ball 60 yards past both of us.

In match-play, in particular, you have the happy feeling of having the upper hand when you launch the ball past an opponent, though it is not quite so much fun when your opponent hits first to the green and you can see his or her ball winking at you from beside the flag.

In stroke-play, the main factor is how your length can affect your par for the course. If, say, a course with a par of 72 includes three par fives of under 460 or so yards which I can reach in two, I should be thinking of my personal par as 69. Also, I will often have the chance of reaching the odd par four from the tee. The first such holes to come to mind are the 289-yard 6th and the 320-yard dog-leg 14th those greens at The Oxfordshire. At the latter, if you go directly for the green, the carry is around 270 yards. I hit both those greens during the course of my win in the 1995 English Open.

No course was ever better cut out for me than the Royal Waterloo in Belgium, where I won my first title as a professional. I was three shots behind Maxime Burton with five to play but, because I could reach each of the three closing par fives in two, I managed to overtake her with an eagle, birdie, birdie finish.

There are more courses in Europe which give me an obvious advantage than there are in the States. On this side of the Atlantic, I will frequently be able to catch the green of a par five with a drive and six iron, maybe less. Over there, a par five is more likely to be the genuine article. Quite often, I will need to hit two shots bang out of the middle if I am to make it. The ultimate challenge is the long 18th at Mission Hills, Palm Springs, home of the Dinah Shore. It is a par five with an island green some 530 yards from the tee. Other than JoAnne Carner, I think I am the only player ever to have reached it. I have done it several times since I first played in that championship in 1988 and, if I had to nominate the finish of my dreams, it would be one of hearing the roar of the crowd as my second shot landed safely on the island. I would then go on to hole for the eagle.

The circumstances were almost but not entirely right in 1994. Leaving the 17th green, I had a one-shot lead over Donna Andrews. Had there been a touch of a following wind, or even no wind at all, I would have reached for my driver on the 18th tee in accordance with the script in my head.

Instead, the wind was slightly against, so I decided to play safe from the tee with a four iron. Safe shot it was not, the ball landing in the right rough. From there, I hit across to the other side of the fairway with a two iron. I was still in good enough shape, but I had to hit my third shot first and I came up with a sadly mediocre eight iron. By the time the ball had stopped rolling away from the hole on that swirling putting surface, I was left with a putt of some 60 yards. Donna, obviously encouraged by what she saw, then deposited her third to within five feet of the flag.

I made a three-putt six and she made a birdie to beat me by a shot. Though 1994 would go on to be a great year, one in which I would win the American Order of Merit, that finish could not have been more of a body-blow. Tony will tell you that he has never known me go so quiet at the end of a tournament.

A good drive, for me, will go anything from 260 to 280 yards but, every now and then, I will find a little extra. There was one time, in Hawaii, in the Kemper Open of 1988, when my drive on a slightly downhill, downwind par five of 559 yards was measured at 341 yards. I reached the green with a five iron.

Another drive which comes back to me from 1988 was the one I uncorked at the US Open at Baltimore at the 558-yard Barn Hole. Two drivers saw me through the back.

More often than not, I will be leading the long driving statistics in America. In fact, at the start of 1995, there was a lovely moment when a Mrs Dottie Sigh in Crystal River pointed out that if the men's and women's long driving statistics had been combined, I would have been lying third overall, my average at the time being, if my memory serves me aright, 269 yards. Having said that, it has to be remembered that the measuring on the two tours at that time was probably carried out on very different holes and in very different circumstances. I don't for a minute think I would be that high among the men.

The subject of my competing alongside them comes up a lot. (I would not be the first. Babe Zaharias did it fifty years ago in the men's Los Angeles Open. She shot a 76, an 82 and a 79 and missed the 54-hole cut.) David Feherty has said he would like to see me playing in a regular men's event, while David Leadbetter once said that he thought I'd definitely be longer than average.

What a lot of people tend not to consider, however, is that were I to play a PGA tour event on a one-off basis, I would be under such pressure to perform that I would be very unlikely to produce my best golf. If, on the other hand, I were to compete in a run of six or seven tournaments, that would be a far more interesting experiment from my point of view. I would have the chance to get into it. But the men would not want it and the moment I sensed as much I would not want to be there.

I touched, earlier, on the fact that that not everything works in favour of the long hitter. I mention this because it will help the shorter hitter to think more rationally when she sees a drive sailing past her own. Even in the context of medal-play, I can honestly promise that there is nothing more irritating to the long hitter than having a shorter-hitting playing companion hitting first to the green and dropping her ball by the pin. If she has hit a four iron stiff, you are then under terrible pressure to get your eight iron closer. Pat Smillie, the former England international, consistently did that to me in one round in France, and I cannot tell you how demoralizing it felt.

There is a second weapon a shorter hitter can bring to bear against a long hitter – a hot putter. You can imagine what it is like to hit two shots aboard the green of a par five, only to find yourself sharing the hole with someone who has made a one-putt four. In my case, the embarrassment of it all will often be rubbed in by my fancying I hear someone saying, 'And to think, Laura was on in two and the other girl wasn't even close!'

Another genuine drawback of hitting a long ball is that you are always having to wait to play your shot. The awkwardness creeps in when you have to explain to your fellow players that you are not going to hit because you think you might reach the green, where the group ahead of you are still playing. They will probably answer that that is fair enough, but you are all the time conscious that you are keeping them waiting and maybe upsetting their momentum. When this situation occurs, it helps if you have a touch of Jan Stephenson about you. The Australian, who has the confidence born of long years of being among the tour's glamour girls, would never allow such considerations to eat into her concentration. She does what is best for her and always has done. That is partly why she has had such a splendid record.

I did myself a real mischief in this way in the 1989 US Open at Indianwood. The 4th hole was a dog-leg of 316 yards, but there was the option of hitting straight for the green, a carry of 270 yards over bushes and scrub. I had caught the green in practice and, thereafter, could not get the idea out of my head; I had these wonderful visions of making a birdie in each of the four championship rounds.

When it came to the highly charged atmosphere of the event itself, I found myself up against the old problem – twin thoughts, each compelling but entirely at odds with the other. I wanted to go for the green, but I did not want to keep the rest of my party waiting.

Each day I kept silent and each day I attempted to drive the green in the knowledge that, were I to come up with the perfect shot, I might ruin things for the trio putting on the green. With such conflicting messages going through my head, it goes without saying that I never got a decent tee shot away at all. Instead of getting my four birdies and being four under par for the hole, I was one over par for the four days. Other professionals who had been content to play the hole as a dog-leg ended up making a much better fist of it than I did.

No one can hit 100 per cent shots when something is preying on the mind. Caution is a killer; it will stifle a shot more than anything else. At club level, as I have mentioned elsewhere, it is a symptom which attaches far more to women than to men. Women, because of all the negative comments foisted upon them all the time, tend to think along the lines of 'I mustn't make a hash of this hole.'

My best drives occur when I have stepped on to a tee knowing precisely where I want to hit. I don't like to have to wait too long before I tee up, because when that happens, the excitement which laces a long shot can be lost. If I am kept waiting, I have learned not to stand there champing at the bit. I will keep away from the hitting area and have a chat with Matthew or my playing companion before tuning into the shot when the time is right.

When I get a good one away, I will feed off the spectators' laughter. While I hate standing up in front of people and making a speech, I like nothing better than to keep a gallery amused with a

LM: Ian Mosey, the professional at The Oxfordshire, spoke after the event of how tough it had been to set up the course for the English Ladies' Open. Though the architect had introduced the various teeing grounds with the emphasis on being able to set the course up to suit the field of the day, Mosey felt that they had two choices in that event: either they could set the course up for Laura, and damage the tournament as a spectacle by leaving the others with too much slogging to do; or they could set it up for the rest of the field and give Laura a head start.

'We chose the latter course,' said Mosey, 'and what it did was to have Laura bypassing a lot of the trouble with room to spare. At the 14th, for example, others were hitting way left before pitching on to the green, which was precisely as the hole was designed to be played from that particular tee. Laura, on the other hand, was able to fly the bunkers and land on the putting surface.'

Mosey said he had not expected Laura to be consistent. He had suspected that her club crossed the line at the top of the swing, and that her long-hitting reputation owed most to the occasional shot dispatched with a touch of draw. In the event, he was impressed with her good, solid hitting and, more than that, the consistency of her strike and shape of shot. Mosey, who describes himself as 'still averagely long' on his occasional sorties on the men's tour, had no hesitation in saying that Laura would hit the ball past him.

To this day, he said, male members who come into his shop recall her tee shots with a kind of nervous laughter.

long tee shot. It does me a power of good to hear their disbelieving shrieks. That kind of support can often set me on a roll in which I play better and better. Last year, for instance, I had that feeling all the way through the Scottish, Welsh and English Opens.

Playing companions, for their part, will usually say nothing beyond 'Good shot!' We are all a bit sensitive in this game, and anything more fulsome would be in danger of being construed as gamesmanship. If, for instance, someone were to say lightly to a long hitter, 'Can't you hit it farther?' it might be interpreted as a remark to make the other start pressing.

IRONS

Though I have seen older ladies who are uncommonly fond of their two irons and contrive to thread the ball down the middle of the fairway every time, I have seen many more women golfers who would do better not to use anything below a four iron. As I have mentioned in the section on woods, it is absolutely pointless to struggle with the lower irons when you can knock the higher woods in close with no bother. Ask Lotta Newmann.

On the other hand, I would not want to convey to a teenager that the low irons are all that difficult. Once you start to do that, you will give the youngster the beginnings of a complex about using these clubs when, essentially, the low iron shot asks for nothing so much as an abundance of confidence. There is a touch of the Rottweiler in the club: it can tell if you are nervous. Confidence apart, it calls for strength, and the teenager who has been bashing a hockey ball about the place is perfectly placed to get to work.

The trouble with most women is that they will bring out a two, three or four iron maybe only once or twice in a round. They then wonder why they do not hit it well. The answer, of course, is that they are not familiar with it. They have no background of success on which to draw; they have no clear-cut picture of what they are trying to do.

The more I have used my two iron, the better a friend it has become. I would go so far as to say that when I take it off the tee, I feel I am guaranteed a spot in the middle of the fairway. That is why I stayed with it off the tee in the Inamori Classic in 1991. My driver had been letting me down, or vice versa, and I was short on confidence. To put away an errant club is a simple solution and, as you know, I am a great believer in simple solutions.

To achieve the kind of bond I have with my two iron, you need to do two things: the first is to watch it hit well by others, such as Bernhard Langer; and the second is to hit it a lot yourself. Vow that whenever you go out to practise, you will give your lowest iron an outing, though remember never to start using it until you are nicely warmed up and into your stride. I am always aghast when I see people starting a practice session with a series of drives. I can guarantee that the next time you go to a driving range, you will see plenty of your fellow golfers starting with a wood, maybe because that is the club they would use from the first tee. You can see the stiffness in the early swings and, as often as not, you can see the player's rhythm go from bad to worse as he or she starts fiddling with grip or backswing in a misguided attempt to put things right. All they needed to do was to give things a chance of clicking into place by working up gradually to the bigger shots.

The best club to use for warming-up purposes is a six iron. I think most people feel at one with their six iron. I use mine for my first 20 or so shots at the start of a practice session, hitting some straight and others drawn or faded as the mood takes me. A point, here: when you hit these practice shots, always have a definite target. Just knocking them down the practice ground will encourage slackness, and is also more than likely to upset the person who wants to set up shop beside you.

Pitches and chips

To my mind, there is not much point in standing there playing hundreds and hundreds of 15–20 yard chips to the same flag. Wherever possible, single out three different flags on the practice green or, if there is only the one flag, improvise with assorted targets of your own. Hit one shot to one, another to the next and so on. Only if you are short on confidence, or working on some point of technique, should you repeat the same stroke over and over.

If you practise nothing other than the same 20-yard chip all the time, the chances are that you will play that particular shot exquisitely when you get on the course. However, what you have got to ask of yourself is how many of those identikit shots are you going to have? Look back at your last round and consider whether any two were the same.

Quite apart from the differing lengths, you are going to have to play one chip one way, another the next. One moment, the shot will ask for a touch of draw, the next, a jot of fade. You have got to be able to knock 'em high, keep 'em low.

For that touch of draw, hood or close the clubhead a shade and have the ball back in your stance. Employ a closed stance by moving your right foot back a bit. When it comes to hitting the shot, picture what you want to do and carry it out with conviction.

For the fade, stand with your feet and club face open and cut across the ball. As with everything from this range, the shot must be crisp rather than floppy and this is something which comes with having real confidence in what you are about. HITTING AND HOPING IS TOO LOOSE A BRIEF. You must be able to 'see' the shot you are about to play.

When you need to hit over a water hazard or greenside bunker, you have a choice. If the lie inspires confidence and the situation calls for a bold shot, you can open your stance and club face and cut the legs from under the ball. If, on the other hand, you want to be rather more conservative, open club face and stance once again but this time apply a slow, full swing. The result will be safe rather than spectacular, with the ball alighting softly.

When it comes to hitting the ball low, hood the face of the club and keep the hands well forward, with the ball back in the stance. That is the shot which will serve you well from, say, the edge of the fairway when you have to keep the ball beneath overhanging branches.

The above is for those who like having it spelt out to a certain extent. For those of you who operate more along the same lines as myself, simply follow the good players as they tackle these different shots on television or on the practice ground. Having watched, mime them in your head and commit them to memory. Then, as soon as possible, go out and give them a try.

To return to the theme about how you practise your chips and pitches, another very good reason for hitting different shots all the time is that you can make the session so much more fun, while all the time you are honing your touch.

Some people – and Jack Nicklaus is among them – stick religiously to the same club when they are practising their short shots. Jack says that he can get more out of practising with the one club for half an hour than he can from using an assortment of clubs for a few minutes each. I am not of that school of thought. I will use a sand wedge one minute, a lob wedge the next. I also make a point of giving myself a variety of different lies, deliberately seeking out tufts of rough grass, together with the odd semi-divot. If you give yourself good lies all the time, you are going to feel cheated when you find yourself in an on-course situation where, literally and figuratively, you're in a hole.

The chip-and-run, incidentally, is not exclusive to the British way of golf, though some would have you believe as much. I will often use it when I am in America. There is no rule to say you can't and there are lots of occasions when it is the better option. In other words, don't leave it behind if you are crossing the Atlantic. If that is how you see the shot on an American course, give it a go, though the heavy nap on the greens is such that you must expect the ball to react rather differently.

I have known people think I'm fooling when I reel off in practice a host of different short shots, and not least when I suddenly throw in a left-handed swing with the club face reversed and the toe of the club brushing the grass. To me, it is all part of developing the necessary feel. I had to employ a left-handed shot at the 18th at Dalmahoy in the Payne and Gunter Scottish Open of 1995. It wasn't the greatest – I hit it a little thin – but it certainly worked very much better than if it had been a first-time effort.

To reiterate, my philosophy is very much one of building up the kind of assurance which goes with having been there before; of having done your homework. That way, you can say to yourself, 'I know I can do that.'

Confidence is the big thing. Gary Player, when he is giving his clinics, often explains to his audience how, if he were to do a person's pitching, chipping and putting for him or her, he would have a 16 handicapper playing to five. On the other hand, were he doing only the driving, he says he could do no better than make that golfer play to ten or thereabouts. That little aside perfectly spells out the importance of the short game.

It's lucky that it is that way round, because everyone has what it takes to improve this part of their play. It has less to do with strength than endless polishing and refining.

Look for the same, easy mastery as you might have with a kitchen implement, a typewriter or whatever. If you are rigid with fear, the exercise becomes twice as difficult. Become familiar with the job in hand, and it's almost second nature. That is how it has become with me in the last few years, and it has made all the difference to my scoring. Nowadays I can often tidy up after a bad shot to the extent that anyone who only saw my card would never know that anything had gone wrong.

Around the green

Though others might be happy enough with an eight or nine iron for the little shots around the green, I mostly stick with a wedge for chips from around the 20-foot range. I carry three wedges – an A wedge with its 56 degrees of loft; a 60-degree lob or pitching wedge, and a sand wedge. Middle and higher handicap golfers can make do with two wedges, but one of the two must be a sand wedge. Women golfers are pretty sensible in the matter of not carrying a ridiculous number of clubs, but the sand wedge should never be omitted. For the majority of bunker shots, it is the only tool for the job.

Your main aim with most of the shorter shots around the green must be to get the ball on the ground as quickly as possible. This is something Ian Woosnam told me a couple of years ago and it is a message which got through. Obviously, there will be occasions when there is an obstacle in your path and the ball needs more time in the air, but there is no point in lofting it unnecessarily. By doing that, you are merely making the shot a more risky affair; there is more to go wrong.

I tend to pluck the 56-degree wedge from the bag for all those chips where there is a fair bit of green to work with. The club face will be square at the set-up and the ball back in the stance. I will be keeping the hands forward and the wrists firm in swinging back and through. A delicate touch is required, but the shots must be crisp, with the clubhead accelerating through the ball.

When there is a fluffy lie, I stay with the same club, open the face and use a little more in the way of wrist action.

Bring out the pitching wedge, or 60-degree wedge, for those occasions when you need to loft the ball a little more. To get the ball up, fast, have it forward at the address, open the club face and put a smooth strike on it. You can stop it uncannily fast with this club, though it is not something you will be able to do at the first time of asking. In fact, it is not a shot to bring out on the course until such time as you have incorporated it in your golfing system by dint of long hours of practice.

The grip must be light, and if that, for some, can seem to be at odds with the instruction to accelerate through the ball, it very definitely is not.

For the tight lie and the slightly longer chip, have the ball towards towards the back of the stance and employ a nice, crisp stroke. As Woosnam says, you want the ball to get down on the ground quickly and start running at the hole.

Some people attach more importance to the direction of the shot than the weight. Myself, I think it far more important to think in terms of getting the weight right. Look at it this way . . . If you are seven feet out in terms of length, you are left with a seven-footer. If, on the other hand, you get the weight right, the same standard of chip which left you seven feet past the hole should leave you something more like a three and a half footer from one side of the hole or the other.

Given 100 chips at a distance of 15–20 feet from the flag, a professional should get down in two about 90 times and maybe hole four of the rest. That is in a practice context. On the course, I would expect my record to be better than that, simply because I can usually manage to find something extra when it really matters.

There are times when I will insist on holing one of these chips before going on the course. More than once, I have made such a fetish of achieving that aim that I've hardly left myself enough time to practise my putting. It is ridiculous, really, but it does give a good idea of how much I manage to make the shots mean to me. If they were meaningless, the session would be correspondingly worthless.

Bunkers

I say this all the time, but the manner in which you walk into a bunker will dictate, to no small extent, whether or not you are going to get the ball out successfully. If you walk wearily into the sand thinking, 'That's done it!' you are likely to mess things up and run up a six or a seven.

It helps if, like me, you actually enjoy bunker shots; but, even if you do not, you should be thinking positively as you step into the trap.

By the time you have made your way to the ball, you should have assessed the type of sand and the shot you will need to play. To quote from Jack Nicklaus's excellent *Playing Lessons*, 'Your feet are great strategic weapons in bunkers. How you should attempt to play the shot depends first on the texture and condition of the sand. The rules forbid you to test it with your hands or the club, but they say nothing about your feet. Use them, along with your eyes, as you walk into the bunker to sense the quality of the sand – its firmness or coarseness, its dryness or wetness. Wiggle your feet into the sand as you address the ball to confirm your initial impressions as well as to build a firm stance.'

Nicklaus goes on to explain that the finer or drier the sand, the deeper the club will automatically tend to dig. 'Think shallow' is what he recommends in these circumstances and what I forgot to do when I found myself in bunkers in the 1995 Weetabix British Women's championship at Woburn, which had the consistency of talcum powder. For the first time in my life, I lost my confidence in sand.

For the bunker shot of 90–100 yards, I am now favouring what Mark McCumber taught me to do during the JCPenney championship of 1995. If the bunker-face permits, I will take a nine iron instead of my sand wedge and play a long, running type of shot. It's easy once you get the hang of it.

For the 50 yard bunker shot, I will nowadays always look to see if there is the chance to catch the ball clean and chip it out instead of playing a conventional bunker shot. A lot of club golfers would never consider doing this, but it would be a useful shot to add to their armoury. I use it a lot.

Moving on to the bunker shot of around 20–30 yards, I will aim well left of target and have my club face open to the extent where it is lying almost flat, looking up at the sky. I swing the club back outside the line before cutting emphatically through the sand. Wherever possible, I follow right through, because that stops me from quitting on the shot. If you think about it, almost every high handicap golfer you see in a bunker will either quit on the shot or else come up with a full, one-pace swing which lacks the necessary zip. The best bunker shots can look lazy but they are deceptive. Bunker shots call for a good, positive strike. As the late Pam Barton used to say, the 'gently-does-it' approach is never going to work.

I do not like to be too precise over what you must and must not do in a bunker. Nothing matters as much as feel, and to get that feel, you have to find yourself a bunker and hit hundreds upon hundreds of bunker shots. You want to try them from the part of the bunker where the sand is at its heaviest and from areas where there is only a thin spread. By the same token, you should have a go from flat lies, upslopes, downslopes – and even from those lies where you are going to have to stand with your feet outside the sand. I cannot stress the advantages of being able to say of an awkward shot, 'I've been here before.'

There are still plenty of courses where there is no practice bunker and, if that applies at your club, you are struggling. However, if you are lucky enough to have one, do make the most of it. That way, you will feel very much less concerned about catching sand than the next person – and that, in itself, will make you feel good.

If I had to nominate the best bunker shot I ever played, it would be the one I had at the 4th hole in my final round when I won in San Diego. The ball was plugged and, to counteract that, I hooded the club and loosened my grip before swinging up steeply outside the line. The hooded face opened as it cut through the sand and the ball came out to a foot – all thanks to Ian Woosnam, who taught me the shot. At that stage of the tournament, everything was very tight, but my par there paved the way for my win.

Finally, if you are setting out to play in one of those five-club competitions, do not even think about leaving your sand wedge behind. For the average golfer to try and escape a deep bunker with anything less than a sand wedge is roughly akin to tackling a bowl of cornflakes with a knife.

PUTTER

I have a hundred putters at home as a legacy of the days when my first move, after a bad putting round, would be to blame the putter rather than myself. Then, three years ago, I took possession of this Maruman putter which rather took my fancy in that it has a face which doubles as a mirror. I remained utterly loyal to this club until March of this year, when I had what can best be described as a three-year itch.

Putting is all about being positive; about kidding yourself into believing that you are putting well and that, even if the ball is not dropping, it is about to do so. In 1988, I had not holed a putt for weeks and was complaining non-stop to Tony – and anyone else who was kind enough to listen – about what a poor putter I had become. Tony could see that I was talking myself out of getting any better and he one day plucked up the courage to say, 'You'll go on putting badly for as long as you keep talking about it.'

That was precisely what happened.

I would not go so far as to say I have convinced everyone else that I'm a great putter, but, for the most part, I have succeeded in convincing myself. And I am the person that matters.

Going back to that three-year itch, it was caused by a missed cut in Tucson. I went to Phoenix the following week without a putter, and what followed was quite a pantomine . . .

All the putter representatives homed in on me on the practice putting green. Would I like a Pip-Squeak? Would I like a V-Line DLR? And so it went on until, in the pro-am, I was attracted to a new Ping Danser which was being used by one of my amateur partners, a man who was part of the Ping organization.

I used it in the first round and it did its stuff. In fact, I had no more than 26 putts and you really cannot argue with that. But, even before the round was done, I knew that the Danser was not going to be my partner the next day.

Round about the tenth hole, I had peered down at its red striped top and its head of wood and brass and thought, 'I don't like the look of you.'

I was tickled to learn that one of the press had reacted to this little tale by saying, 'Who would want to be her boyfriend?'

I am a great believer in an economic putting action. As I putt, I am conscious of making a short backswing and of accelerating through the ball. For years, I used to be relatively better with the shorter putts than the longer ones, but then came Lee Trevino, who told how he had seen me putting some 15–20 footers on television and itched to hold me still. He advised that the best way for me to stop moving was to putt more from the shoulders than the wrists.

A lot of amateurs have unwieldy putting strokes, a fault often accentuated by the fact that, after all their preparation, they have failed to line themselves up correctly and must therefore make compensations in the stroke.

I have an old trick for getting a good roll on the ball: I mark the ball on the green and set it down so that the manufacturer's stamp and number are at the precise point where I will be making contact. In standing there, with my head down, I then visualize the ball running along the correct line and I see, in my mind's eye, the manufacturer's stamp going over and over. It gives me something to concentrate on and it could obviously work for you.

On the short putts, I am of the Jack Nicklaus school of thought in always taking the bold approach, especially under pressure.

Jack summed up his mode of attack in *Playing Lessons* when describing the four-footer he had to make on the 71st hole at Oakmont *en route* to winning his first major as a professional, the US Open:

'The putt was an extremely difficult one with a break first to the left and then to the right, and in holing it I taught myself a lesson that has stayed with me ever since.

'The greater the pressure you are under, the better off you are playing boldly rather than cutely on "must" short putts.

'Deciding that I had neither the nerve nor the delicacy of touch at that stage of the proceedings to read or play a soft, double-breaking putt, I chose to rap the ball firmly enough to negate most of the rolls. I fact, I hit it so hard that the watching Bobby Jones wrote to say, "When I saw the ball dive into the hole, I almost jumped from my chair."'

Tommy Armour had reached the same conclusion years before: 'There may be such a thing as a borrow on a short put, but never anywhere near as much as you think there is, so don't try to nurse the ball along a curved line, figuring on the pull of gravity. If you do, you make the putt too difficult. Go at the short putt like a surgeon operating.'

Armour maintained that the greatest short putter he ever saw was Johnny Revolta. 'Johnny,' he said, 'would walk up to the short putt as though he were saying to himself, "To hell with the line." He would then smash the ball into the hole.'

In my chapter on slow play, I say that the golfer who spends ages over each and every putt is not going to putt any better than the next person. The most positive putters are those who get on with the job in hand; those who do not allow time for negative ideas to take root.

My putting routine is as follows: while my playing companions are putting, if they are putting first, I will be sizing up the green and watching how their balls react. Then, when it is my turn, I will put my ball back where I marked it, plumb-bob and then take a look from behind before adopting my stance.

I will then seek confirmation from Matthew that his reading of the putt is the same as mine and, when I get that, I see it as my cue to take the putter back.

If my putts aren't dropping, I will try putting cack-handed for a few holes. And if that does not work, I have another ploy up my sleeve. I will imitate another player's putting stroke.

That is how I won in Biarritz in 1988. I copied Scotland's Sandy Lyle. Faithfully re-enacting the routine which had helped him to win the Masters and the Suntory World Match Play championship of that year (it was a routine which, along with the stroke, he had based on the Jack Nicklaus method), I just picked a spot to hit over and made the putt with a minimum of fuss.

I have often been drawn into conversations concerning how the men professionals ten to be so much better than the women on and around the greens. The most likely explanation, it seems to me, is that the men have the advantage of playing on greens which are consistently good.

This may be so in the professional arena, but at club level I cannot, for the life of me, understand why a woman should not be the equal of her male counterpart on the putting green. After all, putting does not require anything in the way of brute force.

Finally, if you do make a few good putts in a round, play them back in your head before you go to sleep that night. Putting thrives on positive images, and you must capitalize on every long putt you make. If I am in need of a happy putting memory, I dip into my first win at the McDonald's championship in 1993 – and the ten-footer I made to defeat Sherri Steinhauer. I had the right pace and it slipped in, perfectly, from the right lip. And if I want to draw on a series of successful putts, I go back to the 1992 Solheim Cup. I could not miss that week and, when it came to my single with Brandie Burton on the last day, I drew away from her with a 12-footer at the 14th and a 25-footer at the next.

While you should remember the good putts, there is absolutely no point in dwelling on the bad. Just as Scotland's rugby captain Gavin Hastings refused to be cowed over that relative sitter he missed from almost in front of the posts in the semi-finals of the 1991 World Cup at Murrayfield, so you have got to realize that a missed three-footer is no big deal in the greater scheme of things.

Obviously, if you miscue from that distance to lose a tournament, you are going to kick yourself for a day or so but, if one gets away in the middle of the round, you cannot afford to dwell on it. As Nicklaus has said, if I may draw on one of my particular heroes again, 'Life goes on. Here's another tee, another hole, another challenge. I try to do the only thing that really makes any sense in competitive terms: erase the past from my mind to make room for the present.'

Chapter 7

Managing Mind and Course

THE RIGHT MIND-SET

No less important than how you grip the club is the grip you have on yourself. Tension is the toughest opponent a golfer has. I see it rearing its head in my pro-am partners, and I have often recognized the symptoms in myself.

I have known pro-am partners who have been rigid with fear on the first tee, their arms and legs having about as much flexibility as an ultra-stiff club shaft. When I look at them, I often wonder what they have done in the hours leading up to the starting-time.

If you want to give yourself a realistic chance of playing well on a big occasion, and I cannot see why anyone would want anything less, you need to leave a good hour free before you tee off. It will be an hour in which to get yourself thoroughly organized. That way you will be in a position to approach the first tee with the feeling that you have tied everything up and are now ready to enjoy your day. Muffin Spencer-Devlin is a professional who has had her wilder moments, but I have always liked her suggestion that you should shelve all your worries for as long as you play.

At this stage, as at any other, a quality practice session will reap richer rewards than one in which you hurry through the 50 balls in your practice bag. Take Sam Torrance. Other professionals may go through an entire bucket of balls before going out to play, but he hits just enough to warm himself up and to ensure that everything is in good working order. He's right. If you are swinging well, why go on and on?

I will always start my practice session by hitting a handful of easy shots with my trusty six iron. From there, I will move on to my driver. After that, I will usually hit a few eight irons by way of a prelude to some wedge play. Finally, I sign off with five strikes with a five iron which I hope will be perfect.

After twenty minutes or so, I will move on to chipping and putting. With the chipping, I am seeking to establish that I have plenty of feel in my hands. With the putting, I want to have the sound of the ball dropping in the hole ringing in my ears.

I aim to leave myself time for a leisurely trip back to the clubhouse before heading for the tee. Like most other professionals, I want to be there a good five to ten minutes before my name is called. No one, I make no apology for repeating, should get there too soon. Standing on the tee and watching others ploughing into the undergrowth with their opening tee shots is not going to do anything for your state of mind. Far better to keep intact a mental picture of the glorious drive you plan to dispatch down the fairway. (Incidentally, the same applies if, out on the course, you arrive on the tee of a short hole to find a huge pile-up where players have been hitting into water and needing rulings. Do not get caught up in the spectacle of balls splashing into the depths, because by doing so you would only be imprinting the wrong pictures on your subconscious. Keep well clear and have a conversation about something else.)

If, as used to be the case in some of the amateur events I played, you are joining up with a caddie or trolley-puller for a first time on the 1st tee, now is the moment to get things straight. Apologize for what he or she may see as quirkiness on your part before explaining that you always like to read your own putts, choose your own clubs, or whatever. If it applies, you must also get across the message that you do not like to chat a lot. Far better to say as much at the start than when the bag-carrier in question is in full flow down the first fairway.

In this connection, the story from Lady Heathcoat Amory, concerning her experiences with a noisy steward in the 1929 final of the British championship at St Andrews, is worth an airing.

Because of the swarming spectators on the Old Course that day, each player was allocated a steward. As luck would have it, Lady Amory's attendant walked unnecessarily close and carried on her arm a stiff and crackling mackintosh. More and more, the lady and her mack preyed on Lady Amory's nerves, until finally she said to herself, 'Do I say, "Please move away a little," or do I make up my mind to put up with it?'

On the grounds that any kind of remonstration would affect her concentration, she chose the latter course. And, having made her decision, forced herself to ignore this perambulating distraction.

No less important than your relationship with your caddie is your relationship with your opponent or playing companion. You want to play your 18 holes in the best possible atmosphere, for both your sakes.

So what makes for a good playing companion?

On tour, I loathe playing with people who are loud; people who shout at themselves, their caddies, or the crowd. Dottie Pepper, as everyone knows, is such a player. She gets spitting mad, more hyped up than anyone I know. [But Dottie is Dottie, if that doesn't sound too ambiguous.] Interestingly, Mickey Walker, our Solheim Cup captain, has said that she thinks that Dottie will be keeping a relatively low profile in the match at St Pierre this year. Mickey's feeling is that the British crowds will not put up with her histrionics.

There is another species of playing companion I find difficult to handle. It is the one who starts off by complaining, 'I haven't holed a putt in months,' and then proceeds to make two or three in a row as if from sheer force of habit. That can be extraordinarily irritating.

A variation on that species is the opponent who, when you have her four down at the turn, apologizes for the fact that she is giving you such a poor game. More than once, I have known that kind of remark serve as a turning-point. Also, with such a comment having been made, it is not surprising if the spirit of the match similarly takes an unfortunate twist.

Pat Bradley, one of the more recent entries to the LPGA's Hall of Fame, was a thoroughly disconcerting opponent when I played with her for the first time. She is a wonderful lady, but she disappears into her own little world and you might as well not exist.

I would always be pleased to be drawn with players such as Patty Sheehan, Kelly Robbins or Trish Johnson. Trish and I will chat away for most of the round, maybe about football, maybe gambling.

I like chatting, even with a crowd. The bigger the gallery the better, as far as I'm concerned. The people will help to find your ball, and it is great when they proffer a 'Keep it up!' or a 'Nice putt!' as you are walking between holes. I have never done as well as I should have done in a Weetabix British Open at Woburn, but it is always an exciting place to play. The crowds there long for the English players to do well, and they contribute a lot to the atmosphere.

I don't think anyone has ever summed up sporting behaviour better than Cathy Gerring's father, Bill Kratzert. He always dinned into his daughter that there was nothing finer in golf than to defeat an opponent who was playing at her best. Cathy neither wished a lost ball on her opponent, nor hoped to catch her out on a ruling. That kind of mean-mindedness, which can be so counter-productive, never crept into her play at all.

If you are not letting extraneous things upset you, the chances are that you will be that much more efficient in handling your game. My main fault used to be one of starting to rush when I had a couple of bad shots.

Others will quicken when, say, they do not like the look of a five-footer. They have this notion that the best thing to do is to get rid of it as quickly as possible. Far better to acknowledge that it is an important putt and, having taken that in, to concentrate on putting the best possible stroke on the ball. Then, as I've said elsewhere, get on with the job.

Professionals, in terms of the standard they have attained, have less need to practise their putting than the rank and file, yet they spend a far greater proportion of their practice time on the putting green. Hoping for the best is no substitute for an inner strength born of having done your homework. That inner strength is what worked for Faldo when he had to make that dreadful four-footer in the Ryder Cup at Oak Hill. He hated the look of it, but he overcame the negative vibes to succeed with what many saw afterwards as *the* shot of that momentous Ryder Cup.

Another of my own besetting sins was to moan a lot to myself, or to my caddie, about the bad luck which came my way. When Mark Fulcher talks about my win in the McDonald's championship, he puts it down to the fact that I suddenly saw sense about this.

Once you start feeling sorry for yourself, it is the beginning of the end.

COURSE MANAGEMENT

This skill is not something you can pick up just like that. It comes from years of experience; from long seasons of keeping your eyes and ears open. When, for example, I played with Ian Woosnam at a time when he was at his best, he wanted to know why I had this urge to loft all my shorter shots, even when there was nothing in the way of a bunker between me and the flag. As I mention in my chipping chapter, he told me to develop a lower and less dangerous shot which would get the ball back on the ground as quickly as possible.

Along much the same lines, Seve's example is responsible for the way in which I will often reach for a putter even when I am as much as four or five yards off the green. Not having been brought up on a links, I always used to confine my putter to the putting surface. Seve convinced me that the putt from off the green is often the safer option. Nine times out of a ten, a bad putt will be less destructive than a bad pitch.

On an altogether different tack, Chi Chi Rodriguez furnished another useful tip when he saw me practising. He said that with my shape of shot, left to right, I should always practice from the right-hand side of the practice ground, and thus give myself more room in which to work. After that, I headed for the right-hand side of the practice ground every time.

The same applies when you step on to a tee. The player who hits left to right should tee up close to the right-hand tee box in order to open up the entire fairway, while the player who hits the other way about should set out from the left-hand side of the tee. It is not something you should do unquestioningly, because trees, rough and hazards have to be taken into account, but try it out and get to grips with why it works. No less a teacher than Tommy Armour once said that if you tee your ball up thoughtlessly on all, or most, of the 18 tees, you are likely to produce 'a horrifying addition' to your score.

From what I have seen in pro-am situations over the years, I would say that golfers are very bad at using the shots they have. Nine out of ten people slice. So why do they always aim the ball down the middle and end up in the trees on the right? Why, if they are in the middle of a match or medal round, do they not aim it down the left and cut it into the centre of the fairway? On those occasions when I pluck up the courage to ask, the explanation I am apt to get is that if they aim left and suddenly hit it straight, they will be in trouble.

I practise what I preach in this direction. Though I would trust myself well enough to fade a ball away from trouble on the left, I would never trust myself to draw a ball away from trouble on the right. If there is trouble on the starboard side, I will aim down the left.

You also get a lot of golfers who will step aboard a tee and say, 'I always make a hash of this hole.' By saying that, they are paving the way for a double-bogey or worse. There are plenty of holes dotted around the golfing globe which I do not like, but I long ago learnt how to stop letting them get to me. I will back off a bit at these danger holes, not allow myself to be too aggressive. My driver will be left in the bag and I will produce my 'safe' club, a two iron. With this in my hands, I can more or less guarantee to knock the ball 230 yards down the middle.

My advice, then, is to play the 'bogy' hole in a completely different manner. Instead of persisting in trying to reach the green with, say, a drive and six iron, why not knock a four iron off the tee and take it from there? (I say a four iron because not too many handicap golfers are comfortable with a two iron or a three, and the whole idea of putting away the driver is in order to select a safe alternative.)

When it comes to bunkers, mind over matter is possibly the most important ingredient. In my experience, most handicap golfers people have a fear of even the most straightforward bunker shot. A fear which is totally out of proportion to the task of extricating the ball. For instance, whenever I am playing in a Texas Scramble – an event in which everyone hits from the position of the best drive, etc – I will often recommend playing from a greenside bunker in preference to pitching from a bare lie 50 yards short of the green. I don't think that any group of pro-am partners have ever voted to take me up on the suggestion. Yet, were these people to practise bunker shots to the same degree as they practise their middle irons, they would soon begin to lose that tightening fear.

On the subject of greens, the main problem I see with handicap golfers is that they have little notion of pace. They will have a fair idea of whether to hit right or left of the hole, but often they are completely at sea in the matter of how hard or how gently to hit the putt.

I think we are all too ready to blame bad greens for any putting shortcomings. Far better to accept that a lot of greens will not be in the best of shape and to learn to make the best of a bad surface. As Lee Trevino likes to say, if there was a putting contest across the parking lot, someone would putt well.

I have now had a green built in the garden. It is a two-tier affair, because I am not as good as I need to be on two-tier surfaces. There are not too many opportunities to practise on them, so I reckoned it would help if I had one for myself.

Some of the women on the American tour are excellent in the art of course management. They play a far more considered game than I do. Take Beth Daniel. Where I am never less than aggressive with my shots to the green, she will aim for that point on the green which will afford the easiest putt.

On the subject of chips from the very edge of the green, people will often ask about when and when not to leave the flag in. The basic rule is that it should be taken out if the chip is uphill or flat; left in if the chip is downhill. With any kind of quick chip – one down the grain or on a very slick green – you would do better to leave the flag firmly in place.

To my way of thinking, course management begins long before you arrive on the first tee. There is not a professional alive, for example, who does not worry about his or her opening tee shot.

Some opening drives are inviting enough, but there are others which will flash across your mind about a week in advance. The reason for this first-shot fear is that we are all horribly conscious of the need to get off on the right foot. Not many low rounds follow a horror start.

If the first hole worries me enough, I will do what I do at any 'danger' hole and set out hand in hand with a friend – my two iron.

It is probably asking a bit much of the golfer who plays only for fun to get there in time to go through a serious practice routine. (I myself would not dream of going out and getting properly warmed-up before a game of tennis.) However, it does make sense to take certain steps which will give you a fair chance of getting the most out of your day.

Ideally, you need a few chips to get a bit of feel in the hands; a few putts to remind yourself of ritual, rhythm and sense of pace.

Chapter 8

A Coaching Round

Any coaching I do is usually confined to clinics, many of which are tied up with my Maruman contract in Japan. I would never make a conventional teacher, for I would constantly be telling my pupils that there is no better way to learn than to watch the great players. However, there has been the odd occasion when I have gone out with friends who want me to give them the odd tip. Such an occasion arose while I was staying with the White family in Orlando. I had played with Brian White, the husband, in a pro-am some years ago, and had become friendly with him, his wife Pam and their son Tom.

We had all woken up one sunny morning and felt like nine holes. Brian, a lawyer, was fed up because he had to go to work, but the other two were raring to go, asking if our game could be as much a lesson as anything else.

Pam, aged 43, had a 15 handicap at the time and was determined to get down to single figures. She had a nicely rounded swing but, like so many middle-handicap women, she was inclined to steer the ball rather than make the most of the hit. Yet there had to be some latent power in there somewhere, because I had seen her playing tennis and she had a real swipe to her service. Also, as a part-time physiotherapist, she had strong wrists and arms.

Tom, aged 17 and of coltish build, was playing to seven. In common with many of today's youngsters, he had a good-looking action but, having spent a lot of his time playing basketball and other games, he was not as advanced as some of his golfing peers.

Since he had been making noises about wanting to become a professional golfer one day, Pam was particularly eager that I should have a look at him.

It was, as I say, the perfect morning for golf. As we turned into the car park of the Studio Club, I could see the tops of the trees swaying gently in the direction of the 1st green. I knew that I, for one, was going to enjoy my opening tee shot.

'We couldn't have chosen a better day,' I said.

Pam sensed at once that I was referring to rather more than merely the early sunshine. 'How do you mean?' she asked.

What I mean,' I explained, 'is that we have an encouraging wind to sweep us down the first. Though I usually prefer to hit into the wind, it will be fun to carry the right-hand bunker. I should get home with a drive and eight iron, while you, too, will have no problem in catching the green in two. A driver and a three-wood should do the trick.

Since Pam and Tom had both been keen on this idea of a game-cum-lesson, I told them that I always had a good look at the weather before going out to play. If, for instance, I realized that the first hole was going to involve a stiff and difficult cross-wind, I would start thinking about the shape of shot I would be needing long before I arrived on the tee. It's what I call 'putting myself in the picture'.

Pam asked if I wanted to go to the range first and hit a few balls, but I am ashamed to say that I put her off the idea. This was just a friendly, after all. Having admitted that I was hardly setting the best of examples, I suggested that we should all have a few warm-up swings beside the tee instead.

No sooner had I demonstrated my lack of professionalism in this direction than I needed to pick Tom up on something. In such circumstances, I very nearly decided to let it pass, but then I thought that I would be doing him no favours by keeping quiet.

He was about to take to the course in a pair of trainers and that, to my way of thinking, is the last thing anybody even half-interested in the game should be doing. I asked if he had any studded shoes in the car. 'Yes,' came his reply, but they're not very cool.'

'Cool or not,' I said, trying not to sound too much like a school-mistress, 'you should wear them just the same. You might save yourself a couple of shots. Even the smallest slip of the sole can play havoc with a shot.' I added that the only person I knew who had been able to get away with playing in trainers was Mickey Wright. She won several of her 82 titles on the LPGA tour wearing tennis shoes, but that had nothing to do with wanting to look cool; the lady had a problem with her feet.

Surprisingly eager to please, Tom, all six foot two of him, took himself off to change into proper golf shoes.' On his return, he had a telling glint in his eye as he asked if he and I would be hitting from the same men's forward tees. I said I thought we should and, minutes later, he was offering me the honour.

1st hole

The 1st, at the Studio course, measures 430 yards from an elevated men's tee which serves as a wonderfully inviting stage for an opening tee shot. After my loosening-up swings, I hit my drive as planned, the ball soaring with the wind into the summer sky before dropping on the far side of the bunker. It was a moment to remind me that even if there were no professional tour, I would still want to be playing this game. Maybe they would have me back in the Surrey team.

I only mention my drive because of the bearing it had on Tom's. When he took up his stance and embarked on some serious shuffling, I knew precisely what that meant. He wanted to get his first drive past mine.

It happens all the time when I am playing in pro-ams. Usually, it is because the fellow wants to be able to go back and boast to his mates that he has out-hit me. With Tom, it was more a matter of personal pride.

The shuffling completed, he swung the club as hard as he could, the ball touching down some 150 yards beyond the tee and scuttling into sand. 'Not my best,' he said, a little unnecessarily. 'What did I do wrong?'

Since he had followed me in coming straight to the tee from the car park, I hazarded that it was maybe too early in the round for him to be hitting so hard. He would do better to take things a little more easily.

We walked down the hill towards the ladies' tee, where Pam was rummaging through the top of her bag. Eventually, she emerged, triumphant, with a box of three new balls given to her by her husband, 'on the condition I don't lose them'. I thought to myself how absolutely typical it was for a man to give his wife a new box of balls with so unreasonable an accompanying rider.

I said that she wasn't to worry about losing them – and that if she did, I would give her three more. Her face broke into a conspiratorial smile before she creamed the perfect drive down the fairway on her way to a textbook par.

'Before we go any further,' said Pam, as she picked up her tee, 'can we settle a family argument? Tom says my grip is too strong. What do you think?'

Since nothing had struck me as she drove off, I asked to have another look. Her hands settled comfortably on the club and she showed three knuckles and a little bit more. 'Tom is not wrong in saying that your grip is on the strong side,' I began, in an effort not to contradict him. 'Some teaching professionals would probably say the same, but there are a lot of good tutors – the late Harvey Penick, would have been among them – who would give their seal of approval to your three-knuckle hold on the club. A strong grip means a left-to-right flight and that's the flight which will bring a touch of extra length.

'My own grip,' I continued, placing my hands on her club, 'is supposedly too strong, but it would seem to be right for me . . . 'If your grip is as comfortable as it looks, stick with it. It is certainly not ridiculously far round.'

Pam and I walked up to the aforementioned bunker where Tom was already in residence.

'I'll just make sure I get this one out,' he said.

'Very sensible,' I returned.

That, though, was the only time he exercised his good sense on that hole. When he played his third from much the same place as I had just played my second, he checked that I had used an eight iron before opting for a nine – and forced his shot.

Already, I knew that there was a second piece of advice I needed to impart to young Tom.

2nd hole

The chance arose at the 2nd, a short hole measuring 173 yards.

Since I had made a birdie at the opening hole and thereby retained the honour, I hit first, with my chosen club a seven iron. (We still had the breeze behind us.)

Tom asked, 'Was that a seven?'

When I gave a confirmatory nod, he promptly pulled out an eight. Once again, he swung too lustily, yanking the ball well left of the green.

I asked, lightly, if he and his friends always discussed what clubs they were taking. When he said, 'Yes,' I told him that I used to make that mistake, too. I said that I thought he should work out what he needed for himself. By discussing clubs, and always wanting to be the person taking the shortest iron into the green, he was only adding to the pressures. 'You would do better,' I said, 'to concentrate your energies on the one competition which really matters – your fight against par.'

He listened, politely.

By chance, his mum did precisely the opposite from the women's tee, taking a four iron for her 138 yards when I thought she could very easily have made the green with a five. In her heart of hearts, she clearly felt as much herself, for the shot she struck was oddly apologetic. She had been afraid to hit it too hard.

'Have a go with your five iron,' I said, tossing another ball in her direction. 'Since you've got the right club in your bag, you might as well use it. Hit this firmly and you will be pin high, or just beyond the flag.'

Her blind faith in what I was saying almost frightened me, but she came up with a grand shot which landed within ten feet of the flag.

It was Tom's turn to shine next. His little chip from the semi-rough demonstrated that he was not short of feel. As his mum would do with her first ball, he saved his par. My three was more straightforward but rather less thrilling – a seven iron to ten feet and two putts.

3rd Hole

Hitting first from the tee of the long 3rd, a par five of 470 yards, Tom bisected the fairway with a shot which finished on the edge of the mammoth fairway dip which is the main feature of the hole. Worried about disappearing into the hollow and maybe not having a view of the flag for my second, I knocked a two iron just short of his ball. Pam, too, got a good one away and, as we walked down the fairway, I asked Tom about his golfing plans. He told me that he would be applying for a college golf scholarship. He wanted to get a degree in business studies and to try for his American tour card as soon as he had finished.

I explained to Tom and Pam that I wasn't the best person to advise on the American college scene. I would probably have followed that route had I lived in the States but, back in England, there was another way.

I told them of the thriving amateur circuit in Britain; of stroke-play tournaments, match-play tournaments and umpteen team tourneys which, in contrast to American college golf, are all match-play. Among the team contests, I listed county matches and county weeks, Home International matches at junior and senior level and, of course, the Curtis Cup – Great Britain and Ireland versus America.

When Tom asked if all that match-play had any relevance when it came to the professional game, I came up with a counter-question. 'What about the Solheim Cup?'

I then reeled off my theory about match-play teaching you to go for your shots in a way you seldom can with a card and pencil in your hand. In contrast to what can happen in stroke-play, the odd bad hole in a match is not going to matter overmuch.

I mentioned that the reason I had chosen the British amateur path was because I wanted to base myself at home for as long as possible before embarking on the professional trail. I detailed how, in the winter months, I used to look for employment in the supermarket or the local bookmaker's, and how, to my mind, such a background had contributed to the fact that I so enjoy my golf today. 'There are plenty of girls on tour,' I ventured, 'Who have never done any of life's more mundane jobs. As a result, they never appreciate just how lucky they are to be able to play golf for a living.'

Tom wanted to know how a person could tell if he or she had what it takes to turn professional.

I stressed that it wasn't just a matter of hearing from others that you are good enough. You have to prove to yourself that you can win. When girls at home ask me to elaborate, I say that they should not attempt to make the switch without first having played for their national side – the English, Irish, Scottish or Welsh. Preferably, they should make a British team as well, especially if they are from one of the weaker nations.

I told Tom that he had plenty of time and that college golf, with its cluttered golfing calendar and emphasis on stroke-play, would give him a very good idea of whether he was cut out for the professional scene. I also gave my approval, for what it was worth, to his idea of doing business studies. There is far more paperwork involved in being a professional golfer than most would believe possible. If he could tackle all that competently, he would have one less worry on his mind. There were plenty of young professionals, I told him, who had been taken to the cleaners by unscrupulous managers – managers who took advantage of the fact that their charges did not have a clue about money.

Tom nodded and I turned my attention to my second shot. It was me to hit first. I took my two iron out again and it turned out to be perfect or, to be more precise, a foot away from being perfect.

I suspected that Tom would have liked me to have said what I had hit, but I wasted no time in slipping the iron back into the bag. He wheeled round and got on with things for himself. He had got the message.

I made a three, Tom a four and Pam a five. She was in charge of sorting out the strokes and, by her reckoning, she was one up on both of us, while I was one up on Tom. (For the record, I was giving Pam a stroke a hole and Tom a stroke at the even holes. Tom, meantime, was giving Pam the same every-other-hole allowance as I was giving him.)

4th Hole

It was Pam's turn for a lesson down the par-four 4th, a hole of 360 yards for the men and 335 yards for the women.

There are assorted bunkers dotted across the fairway from around what is the 190-yard mark from her tee, but that did not stop her from pulling out her driver. 'Hang on a minute!' I called, grateful for the fact that she was not in the mould of an Alison Nicholas or an Annika Sorenstam, for the pair of them are liable to have hit before you have had time to blink. Pam looked up.

'Why are you taking your driver here?' I asked. 'Surely, you're in danger of catching one of those traps?'

She wanted to assure me that she had not pulled it out unthinkingly. Rather was it was something she did every time on the grounds that her chances of catching one of the traps was no more than fifty-fifty. There were plenty of good lies to be had on the ground between the hazards.

I asked her why she didn't hit a three wood off the tee in order to take the bunkers out of play and to give herself a trouble-free second into the green.

'Ah!' she said, by way of indicating that she had the answer to this one, too. 'If I take my three wood, I will be left with around

145 yards to the green. That would ask for a four iron and I'm not very confident with my four iron.'

'I have another idea,' I ventured. 'Why not hit a four wood off the tee and another four wood on to the green?'

It was a compromise which would work and one which, according to her gleeful calculations, paved the way for her to be two up both on Tom and me as we moved across to the 5th tee. She did not say as much, but she had in fact matched the women's par at every hole – 4,3,5,4. Not at all bad for a 15 handicapper.

5th Hole

The 5th is a short hole of 130 yards. Because of the inordinate amount of divots which had been taken during the holiday spell, they had put down mats both for the men and the women. As is so often the case, these were not properly aligned. Neither was far out; just enough to have all three of us feeling thoroughly uncomfortable at the address.

Tom never did get lined up correctly and wound up pushing his iron into the bunker on the right of the green.

I suggested that Pam should go next, partly on account of her success at the previous hole and partly because she was ready to play. She reacted to the awkward teeing situation by hitting long before she was ready to hit – ot at least that was what I thought.

She was to confirm as much: 'I know from experience that the longer I stand on a tee like this, the less chance I have of hitting the thing,' she said, shaking her head as her ball took a last-minute tumble into Tom's bunker.

As I teed up, I gave them a step-by-step account of how I was trying to keep the mat out of my consciousness. Since every thread of it was doing its level best to throw me off course, I had picked out a prominent tuft of grass in front of the mat and superimposed an imaginary line between that and my ball. That was the only line I wanted to know about.

'Mind over matter,' I said, by way of talking myself into playing a good shot. It worked.

While we were stepping towards the green, my attention was drawn to activities in the rough at the adjacent 8th. A burly gentleman, whom I had met before, was peering through a broken branch at his ball. 'Hey, Laura!' he called across, cheerfully. 'What can I do with this?'

I always dread being called in to officiate but, since he was clearly playing nothing more than a bounce-game, I walked across. The branch had parted company with the pine tree above, probably during the electric storm a couple of nights before. It was a good six foot long and needed someone to take a saw to it before it could be removed.

To my relief, I knew the ruling here. We had had it drawn to our attention in an LPGA tournament after a night of high winds. Namely, if a part of a large branch which has fallen from a tree (and is thus a loose impediment) interferes with a player's swing, the player may break off the interfering part rather than move the whole branch.

He was delighted at that piece of news and set about snapping off the section above his ball.

'What happens if his ball moves while he's doing all that?' asked Pam, not unreasonably.

'He will be penalized,' I replied, before pulling out my *Rules of Golf* in order to substantiate what I was saying.

'Here we are,' I said. 'Rule 18-2 c:

'*Through the green, if the ball moves after any loose impediment lying within a club-length of it has been touched by the player, his partner or either of their caddies and before the player has addressed it, the player shall be deemed to have moved the ball and shall incur a penalty stroke. The player shall replace the ball unless the movement of the ball occurs after he has begun his swing and he does not discontinue his swing.*'

Pam and Tom both volunteered that they would not have had a clue how to advise our friend in the rough. I voiced my thoughts about there being far too many rules before advising the two of them to take time to leaf through the pages of *The Book of Rules* and *Decisions on the Rules of Golf*. I was not saying they should learn them off by heart; I just felt they should try to become *au fait* with where to find things.

I was interested to see how Pam and Tom would make out in their bunker. Both had adequate lies but very little in the way of green to work with. They were going to have to stop their balls very quickly. Pam, playing first, stabbed at hers, leaving it in the trap. Without so much as pausing to address her third, she did the same again. And again.

'Stop, stop!' I exhorted her. 'Just because you left your first attempt in the bunker, there was no need to panic. I took two to escape a trap when I won my US Open. It doesn't have to be the end of the world.

'Either do what Scotland's Belle Robertson used to do and walk out of the bunker before your next attempt, or have a few deep breaths. Then, when you start again, remember to hit right through the shot rather than at it.'

Though she could have done with a touch more acceleration on her downswing, she came out well enough leaving herself a six-footer.

Tom, for his part, brought a better attitude to the task in hand. He was not remotely scared of bunkers, because he and his friends were forever fooling around in the club's practice trap. He could have been a professional, the way he handled that one.

I could see that Pam was a bit embarrassed at those goings-on in the sand but I told her that she should not feel rushed into making an even bigger hash of things. 'You've still got the chance of escaping with nothing worse than a six,' I reminded her. 'Take your time.'

She calmed down and made the putt. I told Tom that there was a lesson there for both of us, and then owned up to having had terrible rushing fits of my own – fits which went on well into my professional career. Some people used to put it down to the pressure, but I was never convinced. For example, I noticed that there were days when it would take nothing more than a thinned bunker shot and subsequent bogey to precipitate one of my crazed spells.

I rather think a psychologist might have agree with my theory that, deep down, I was trying to make a quick getaway from trouble. There were times when it worked, times when it manifestly did not. However, to give an illustration of the former, I was five over par after seven holes in the 1988 Weetabix British Women's championship at Lindrick but still contrived to hand in a two-under-par 70.

6th hole

On to the 6th, a par five of 460 yards where Tom hit his ball into long rough. He had swung well enough but had aimed too far left. I mentioned that it would be worth his while, when practising, to put down a club across the front of his feet, simply by way of checking up on his alignment.

Pam and I were wandering up the middle of the fairway chatting about this and that when Tom's voice wafted across. 'Did you see where my ball went?' he asked.

I called back that he was looking a good twenty yards beyond where it had gone in.

'I can't think,' I said to Pam, 'why Brian should worry about you losing golf balls. He should be more concerned with Tom. He didn't begin to notice where he hit his drive.' Pam muttered that most of the youngsters she knew seemed to be the same. Her theory was that because they played so much with adults when they were starting out, they expected the adults to do the watching for them.

Since Tom was still not having any luck, I walked across and found the ball just like that. He looked at me as a child might look at the magician who has produced a rabbit from under his hat.

'If you want to know my secret,' I said, 'I not only watched the ball but noticed that it was on the same line as the azaleas.'

After he had hit back on to the fairway, I told that him that the whole business of looking out for your own and others' golf balls was a perfect illustration of that biblical saying about doing unto others as you would have done unto you: 'If you keep an eye open

That expression is usually detonated by slow play! (November 1968)

All that is wrong with me here is that I've been
made to put on a dress. (At school, age 5)

The school netball team. I'm smiling broadly enough but it still hurts that I was never given my colours in any school sport.

The Surrey team at the divisional county finals, Chigwell, 1982. *Back row, left to right*: Winnie Wooldridge, Jill Nicholson, Laura Davies, Catherine Bailey, Diana Walpole, Sandy Cohen. *Front Row, left to right*: Sue Birley, Joan Rothschild, Diane Bailey, Jill Thornhill.

Standing outside Royal Birkdale with the Weetabix British Open trophy in 1986.

My father had been smoking non-stop throughout the week but he finally relaxed enough to put down his cigarette and help me lift the U.S. Open trophy aloft, 1987.

St. Mellion, August 1987. In this family picture, my stepfather, Mike, and my mother, Rita, are holding the candlesticks that were my prize for winning the 1986 British Women's Open. My brother, Tony, is helping with the 1987 U.S. Open trophy which I had just brought back from Plainfield. My cousin, Matthew Adams, is on the right.

Leaderboards that tell a magic story. This was Toledo, where I managed to get the better of my great heroine, Nancy Lopez, 1988.

Playing in Japan with Ayako Okamoto, 1989.

My favourite picture of my brother, Tony, in the days before he switched from being my caddie to my manager.

These are a few of my favourite things... my house, a couple of cars and my two dogs, Ben and Dudley. I bought the Triumph convertible more for sentimental reasons than anything else. My first car was a Triumph and when it was written-off I always yearned for another. This one was sold to me by a member at West Byfleet and I had all the fun of getting it restored. (*Phil Sheldon*)

My favourite old leopard-print shirt. I dragged it out on lots of last days and it usually came up trumps. Weetabix Women's British Open, 1995. (*Mark Newcombe/Visions in Golf*)

What else but the winning Solheim Cup side of 1994. *Back row, left to right*: Helen Alfredsson, Trish Johnson, Catrin Nilsmark, Mickey Walker (captain), Laura Davies. *Middle row, left to right*: Kitrina Douglas, Lotta Neumann, Florence Descampe. *Front row, left to right*: Pam Wright, Alison Nicholas, Dale Reid. (*Mark Newcombe/Visions in Golf*)

A winning moment in the 1994 Solheim Cup. (*Mark Newcombe/Visions in Golf*)

Winning my second major, the
McDonald's LPGA in Dupont, 1994.
(*Simon Bruty/Allsport*)

The Evian Masters, 1995. I managed to win in Evian in 1995 and 1996. After the
1996 event, I found myself criticized in a magazine for having taken a peep at the
England–Spain football match during the last round. I had a miniature television in
my bag and I simply had to know the score! Some people who don't understand
how crazy I am about sport thought it was bad form. (*Phil Inglis/Allsport*)

Sharing a triumph with my partner, Alison Nicholas, in the 1992 Solheim Cup at Dalmahoy. (*David Cannon/Allsport*)

One of my favourite venues in all golf: Palm Springs for the 1995 Nabisco Dinah Shore. (*David Cannon/Allsport*)

I can never resist a good game of cricket. We take a bat and stumps round the States and often play with the caddies in the evenings. The Americans think we are mad! (*Simon Bruty/Allsport*)

I assume there was some sand left. Bunkered, 1992. (*Mark Newcombe/Visions in Golf*)

1 At the set-up, I agree with what others say about my standing nice and tall to the ball. That helps to get the straight line of the left arm and club which is a simple, easy-to-find starting position.

2 Johnny Miller, when he analyzed my swing, drew attention to the way I slide off the ball so my head is over my right knee. I am under the impression that much of my power comes from this slight sway.

5 Everyone tells me I drop my head a little at this point, but I have the feeling that I make up for this by being on my toes. I am ready to pounce.

6 Anyone who follows women's golf closely is almost bound to comment on how much longer my head stays down than Annika Sorenstam's. Her head has already started to rear at this point and that's right for her.

3 As I have said in the text, if you look at the top of the swing, the power almost shows. Here, I am still looking at the back of the ball and am not conscious of any kind of pause before the downswing.

4 Johnny Miller is not alone in having likened the cupping of my wrists to John Daly's, but I see myself as simply adopting the best position from which to hit the ball hard.

7 Head still well down with what the experts all call 'a good extension' through the ball. I like the fact that everything still looks so controlled at this stage. It suggests a good, solid shot.

8 A nicely balanced finish and one that says I am at ease with the shot. Some people say it doesn't matter what happens once you have hit the ball, but I think a bad finish and a bad swing go together.

Another view of a Laura drive (*J. D. Cuban/Allsport*)

1

2

5

6

3

4

7

8

I don't think I've held back on this particular shot! *(Mark Newcombe/Visions in Golf)*

for your playing companion's ball, he's going to feel duty bound to keep an eye open for yours.'

I mentioned to Tom that there was another factor to be taken into account. Namely, that the golfer who doesn't bother to watch his ball will be making those around him cross on two counts. Though no one minds looking for a genuinely lost ball, no one wants to have to break his concentration every few minutes to embark on a search which could have been avoided. On top of that, people who play at a decent pace don't want to be slowed down to the point where they will worry about holding up those behind.

Tom muttered something about never having been any good at finding balls. I told him, a little sharply, that he wasn't likely to improve until he practised the art.

After putting out at the sixth, Tom and I asked Pam to recap on the matter of how things stood. Apparently, I was level with both of them.

'You've forgotten something,' said Tom to his mother.

'What's that?' said Pam.

'Just that you're two up on me,' he replied.

Pam seemed touched that he had bothered to work it out.

7th hole

The 7th is not my type of hole. It measures 400 yards and has trees encroaching on both sides of a narrow fairway. If anything, it reminds me of the Duke's Course at Woburn where, year after year, I tangle with the woods during the Weetabix British Women's Open.

Tom hit a fearless drive down the middle. I took my two iron and blasted it into much the same position as his. A good shot in the circumstances. Pam, like me, had the feeling that this was a somewhat claustrophobic hole. She steered the ball into a patch of muddy undergrowth just beyond the semi-rough on the right. When we got there, her ball was half caked in mud.

'How can I tell it's mine?' she asked.

Tom informed her that she could pick it up for identification purposes, but I knew, from experience, that that was not entirely right. I dragged out the rule book again. 'Here goes,' I began.

'Except in a hazard, the player may, without penalty, lift a ball he believes to be his own for the purpose of identification and clean it to the extent necessary for identification. If the ball is the player's ball, he shall replace it. Before lifting the ball, the player must announce his intention to his opponent in match-play or his marker or a fellow-competitor in stroke-play and mark the position of the ball. He must then give his opponent, marker or fellow-competitor an opportunity to observe the lifting and replacement.

'If he lifts his ball without announcing his attention in advance, marking the position of the ball or giving his opponent, marker or fellow-competitor an opportunity to observe, or if he lifts his ball for identification in a hazard, or cleans it more than necessary for identification, he shall incur a penalty of one stroke and the ball shall be replaced.'

Pam said 'Wow!' before going on to observe the correct procedure. The muddied missile did indeed belong to her. Now she had the unenviable task of trying to hit it out. 'Should I deem it unplayable?' she asked.

'I don't think so,' I said. 'It's more unpalatable than unplayable. If you give it a good whack you can get back on the fairway.'

Pam said she felt at her strongest when armed with a nine iron. I agreed that she had the right club and advised her to grip it a little tighter than normal in order to allow for the interference of the weeds as she came into the shot.

'Hit it hard,' came my final instruction.

She hit it a whole lot harder than I expected, the ball skipping out on to the cut grass. On the green in three, she made a five against Tom's four and mine.

'You're pretty good on your rules,' said Pam, as we departed the green.

'Part of the job,' I replied, before reiterating that I could not be congratulated on anything more than knowing where to look.

There were some professionals, I said, who came close to knowing them by heart.

8th hole

The 8th hole, 380 yards from the men's tee, involved a run-of-the-mill drive followed by a carry over water in front of the green. With Pam's tee well in front, the three balls finished up in a row, waiting to be smacked over – or maybe into – the water.

The conversation returned to the professional scene and Pam was asking how I managed, financially, when I started out. I told her about the £1,000 my mum and stepfather had given me and of some early sponsorship I had from IBM. I recalled, too, how I finished second in what was only my second outing as a professional. 'I was one of the lucky ones,' I explained. 'I know plenty of others who have had a real struggle to get started.'

I was thinking, at this point, of Scotland's Myra McKinley. Coached by Sam Torrance's father Bob, this gifted Scot had played a key role in the 1994 Curtis Cup at Chattanooga and turned professional not long afterwards. She made a promising enough beginning but, soon after, was having to cut down on the number of tournaments she could play because of the expense of travelling from her home on the Cowal Peninsula. By all accounts, her every journey begins with a trip on the ferry. It struck me as very sad that someone so obviously talented was having so many enforced interruptions at a time when she was otherwise so well equipped to get to grips with her trade.

'Ideally,' I said to Pam, 'you need to have enough money at the start to allow you to be patient. There are players, like Colin Montgomerie, Bernard Gallacher, Ben Crenshaw, Seve Ballesteros and José-Maria Olazabal, who are successful very quickly, but there are plenty more who take ages to break through.

In Britain, I told them, the name which would spring to everyone's lips was Carl Mason. Though he had a handful of second-place finishes under his belt, Carl did not win his first tournament, the Turespana Masters Open at Montecastillo, until he was 40. After a ten-under-par 278 which left him two shots ahead of Olazabal, he admitted that he had thought he would never do it. Four months later, Carl won again, his second title none other than the Scottish Open at Gleneagles.

Among America's later starters, I named Larry Nelson, who had never played golf until his wife gave him a set of clubs for his 22nd birthday. For the record, he has three majors to his name.

We were now up to the three balls and it was Pam to play first. The shot called for her three wood, but she protested that she loathed to use it without a tee peg. I told her that I knew what it was like to have a thing about a club and mentioned my major falling-out with my driver in the early 1990s.

'I'll tell you more about that in a moment,' I promised. 'For now, take your trusty four wood and bang it into the mouth of the green.' She followed instructions to the letter.

I liked the look of Tom's shot. It finished 15 feet to the left of the hole. Heaven knows whether it was by accident or design, but he had arrived on that side of the hole which offered the easier, uphill putt. I just managed to put mine inside his, but not by much.

Our conversation about falling out with various clubs resumed. I told Pam about how I eventually got back on good terms with my driver by playing through the pain barrier. I went several weeks of hitting the most dreadful shots but, gradually, there were more and more good ones sandwiched between the bad. The moment I knew I had things conquered was when I won the European Ladies' Open. Towards the end my driving was beginning to disintegrate anew, and my lead was disappearing fast, but I managed to hang on.

I said to Pam that there was an easier way back for someone such as herself who wasn't trying to play tournaments all the time. She should wait for one of those days when she felt at peace with the world and give the four iron and/or the three wood an outing on the practice ground in among her favourite clubs. 'A lot of people,' I said, 'make the mistake of just taking out the club which is doing them a mischief. Because they aren't comfortable with it, they are edgy from the start. They don't begin to find their rhythm and are inclined to make things worse rather than better.'

We walked from the green with three fours, a fact which was not lost on Pam's husband, Brian, who had strolled out to watch us finish.

'How is it,' he asked Pam, 'that when you play with me you always hit into the water?'

I could have answered that one for him but, discretion being the better part of valour, I desisted.

9th hole

We sorted out where we stood on the 9th tee. Pam had beaten Tom by 2 and 1, while the two of them were both one up on me.

The closeness of our little match, coupled with the fact that we now had an audience, brought a new measure of pressure to the proceedings.

The 9th is a hole of 390 yards which asks for a good, solid drive to hold the left side of the fairway as opposed to rolling into the gaping gap to starboard. Go down in that dip and you have to hit a second over a pair of cross-bunkers which look for all the world like a wall. Only the very tip of the flag will be visible above.

From the left side of the fairway, on the other hand, there is a good enough view, even if the second shot still has to be deadly accurate. If too far right, it will kick into the aforementioned bunkers; if too far left, it will tumble into a little gully running all along that edge of the green.

The drives were no problem and, as we walked up to them, we discussed practice. Pam said she set aside two half-hours a week, using one for her chipping and another for everything else. That, she stressed, was in addition to the 20 minutes or so she would put in before each of the three 18-hole rounds she would normally play in a week.

Tom said that he tended to play rather than practice. He did not get much time for golf during the school term, but he was on the course every day in the holidays, competing in all the club's junior and senior events and playing with his friends the rest of the time.

I told them that I too was more player than practiser, though I did explain that I had practised a lot in my teenage days. Far more than most people are apt to give me credit for.

We all had some thinking to do when we got to our seconds. Pam, who had had a 20-yard start from the tee, needed everything she had got for hers. With the three wood still out of favour, she opted for the four, but admitted that whatever she played, she was never going to feel terribly confident at this minefield of a hole. I suggested she try Tony Jacklin's old trick. When he didn't like the look of what lay immediately ahead – maybe a cliff-top or a cavernous water hazard – the former British and US Open champion would take aim on, say, some some distant steeple.

Pam selected the window of the ladies' lounge in the clubhouse and it worked a treat. Her husband's jaw dropped as her ball ran round nicely on to the putting surface. Tom hit what I thought was a bit of a risky shot, a towering six iron over the corner of the left-hand trap. It finished a foot over the bunker's bank and ran up to six feet.

'Very good,' I said, 'but, for myself, I'm going by your mother's route.'

I punched a shot to the left side of the green and it swirled with the slope to five feet.

Pam putted her 20-footer to 'gimme' distance for a net birdie. She had beaten me.

Now Tom had a six-footer which would enable him to match his mother's win.

I watched with interest. Would he be one of those who tackle a pressure putt too quickly, or would he be like that mythical fellow who stared at his putt from so many different angles that he eventually picked it up on the grounds that he could no longer see any possible way to hole it?

Tom came close to falling into the latter category. He studied his six-footer as one who had never clapped eyes on a six-footer in his life. He looked from behind, from in front, from on top, from every angle on the clock. And the longer he looked, the more the tension mounted.

He cracked a joke and smiled when at last he took up his address but I could tell, from the stranglehold he had on the grip, that his chances of making this putt had receded. The late Henry Longhurst, when he was moved to comment on the extraordinary lightness of Bobby Locke's putting grip, asked the South African how he would hold the putter if he had a three-footer to win the Open.

'Lighter still,' Locke replied.

I would have put good money on Tom leaving his putt short and that's what he did, though only by a whisker rather than the six inches I had anticipated. It looked as if the ball might topple in and he stood over it, doing his best to persuade it to drop.

'Come on,' said Pam. 'We can't wait all day.'

'We can't wait longer than ten seconds,' said I, hurriedly invoking the rule which could save me from defeat.

Tom laughed before tapping the ball in for his four.

His last hope of beating me evaporated when, thank heavens, I knocked in my five-footer.

19th hole

The drinks were on Pam who, we worked out, had covered the nine holes in 40 against the par of 36. In other words, in spite of her terrible 5th hole, she had played to a handicap of eight.

I remarked that she could do with some more informal practice in bunkers. She was too statuesque in the sand. If she were to empty a bagful of balls into the practice bunker once a week or so and knock them all out from good lies and bad, she would not take long to become a lot more confident and familiar with the shot.

In fact, my verdict was that she was not hitting enough shots with most of her clubs. I asked her to work out roughly how many times she used her four iron in a week, and she had quite a shock. She said she probably hit about ten practice shots and a total of six shots on the course. 'No wonder you have trouble with it,' I ventured. 'You don't even know it.'

In her case, I was prepared to predict that she would be down to single figures before I was back at the end of 1996.

Brian, on his own admission a totally unambitious golfer, was delighted to hear so encouraging a report on his wife. He wondered if he should pay for her to have more lessons.

'Not necessary,' I said, 'but there is something you could do.'

'What's that?' he asked, interested.

'When you give her a new ball,' I instructed him, gently, 'couple the gift with a positive message. After all, a ball is only a ball.'

He gave Pam a fond look and vowed to change his ways.

The conversation then turned to Tom. I said that I liked the way he played but that he still had a lot of work to do if he wanted to be a professional. His holiday golf was obviously serving him well, but it was my impression that he needed to start doing a lot more in the way of regular practice, and that he had to keep it going during the term-time. I went on to recommend that if he, like me, tended to find practice sessions a bit of a bore, he should set himself challenges which would turn them into fun.

I asked Tom something I had meant to ask him out on the course. Had he gone out to watch the professionals when they were in town for the PGA tour event two weeks earlier? He told me that he had not had the time because he had been busy playing himself. I did not mind saying that I thought that was a mistake. Golfers are never better at imitating others than when they are young, and I was sure that he could have picked up all sorts of little touches and absorbed some of their rhythm.

'Who's your favourite player?' I asked him.

'You are,' said he, effectively putting an end to that little lecture.

Chapter 9

Slow Play

Professional golfers need to think long and hard about what they are doing to the game. I know what Bernard Gallacher said at the Ryder Cup at Oak Hill about professionals thinking of the future while amateurs live in the past but, if the professionals – men and women alike – don't get a move on, they don't deserve to have a future. The pace at which most of them play is deadly.

Bernhard Langer and Nick Faldo are the main culprits on the men's tour, with Langer the slower of the two. The pair of them were playing alongside each other as Faldo took 43 to reach the turn on the second day of the 1995 Million Dollar tournament at Sun City. Langer was speaking in all seriousness when he afterwards noted how Faldo, with all his problems, had made them fall behind. That struck me as a bit rich when I read it!

If Faldo was always going to scoff at the idea of Langer calling him slow, the Englishman must surely have taken a bit of notice of Mark O'Meara in the Mercedes championship at the start of 1996. When he and Faldo were warned, O'Meara pointed an accusing finger at his playing partner and said, 'If he's playing slowly, it has nothing to do with me. Nick said he was running but I was watching him and thinking to myself, "Why on earth do you stand over the ball so long before you hit it?"'

For obvious reasons, the foremost of which is that it is not my job to do so, I am not going to make the mistake of naming names among my sister professionals on the women's tours. Let me just say that 80 per cent of them – and that is a conservative estimate – are on the slow side.

When I was an amateur, a stroke-play round would take three to three and a half hours – maybe four in bad weather. Today, our rounds on the professional tour average out at around five hours, and they are getting slower. We were on the course for five and a half hours at a time at last year's US Open at The Broadmoor. I remember my first round with Ayako Okamoto and JoAnne Carner. Ayako and I chatted the time away, but for JoAnne, who is in her mid fifties, it was too much. She timed the wait on the 3rd tee at 23 minutes and said that it had spelt the end as far as her momentum was concerned.

In Britain, things reached their nadir at last year's Welsh Women's Open at St Pierre. There was one day when there were as many as four couples trying to play the 5th, a par four with a witches' caldron of a cavity short of the green. There were all kinds of problems brewing all the time and not enough officials on hand to sort them out. I think it was in the second round that someone passed me one of those wooden Quiet Please boards and we had a makeshift game of cricket.

Play was miserably slow again at the 1995 Weetabix British Women's Open at Woburn, with group upon group piling up on the 18th tee, a par five where some competitors needed to wait for the green to clear before hitting their seconds. Several of the Americans availed themselves of the hot dog stand at the 17th green and said that it made sense to have lunch there rather than back at the clubhouse.

At Woburn, the usual problems were exacerbated by the fact that too many different bodies were in charge of giving rulings. The Ladies' Golf Union, the R&A and the women's tours all provided officials. When a player did not like what she was told by one of these parties, she would simply call for a second opinion from another.

Karrie Webb, the eventual winner, did just that. She asked for a ruling when she caught a hole in the bank which falls away from the right-hand side of the 12th green. Geraldine Turner from the

LGU was with her group and gave the correct ruling, but Karrie wanted to hear it from one of the professional administrators. When one of the European Tour officials took over, he merely endorsed what Mrs Turner had said – namely, that the Australian's only way out of the hole was to play the shot as it lay. There were no signs of burrowing animals; it was a little hollow formed by contorted tree roots.

What most professionals fail to appreciate is the effect their slow play has on others. In the first place, they are ruining things for spectators. People pay good money to come through the gate, but there must be days when they are bored out of their minds. If they have had a miserable time, they are hardly going to go back to their clubs and say positive things about the women's tour to their friends. I remember being somewhat alarmed at an English Open at Tytherington in the not-too-distant past when a party of golfers from the Midlands came for a day out and left early. They said that things were so slow as to be 'unplayable' from their point of view. I could only sympathize with them.

As often as not, there is a television audience out there suffering as well. I know myself that when I am watching golf, it is maddening when they end coverage at the 16th or 17th because the players have fallen behind. The women professionals, unlike the men, are still courting the television people, and it is crazy for us to risk antagonizing them in the way that we do.

Slower-moving professionals also set an appalling example to amateurs who, inevitably, take their lead from the golfers they see on television. If they watch Faldo fussing interminably over a putt, they will do the same. Half the time, the higher-handicap golfers won't even know what they are really looking for as they scan the green from one side and then the other before invoking the plumb-bob method. If you watch a higher-handicap golfer going through the motions, you will notice that by the time he gets to tackle the putt, his grip will have become impossibly tight. With a tight grip, he will have little chance of getting the pace of the putt right.

Besides getting tense, he will have allowed time for doubts to take root.

You are either going to miss a putt or you are going to hole it. Though you obviously need time to get organized, taking longer than the next person does not mean that you have a better chance of getting the ball to drop. Quite the reverse, in my experience.

It is not just on the greens that the professionals' lives are apt to come to a virtual standstill. The trouble starts long before then. Just watch the puppets, as I call them, as they wait to hit to a green. In many cases, they will not even begin to consider the shot in hand until the putting surface is clear.

What they should be doing, of course, is to get all their grass-tossing and yardage calculations out of the way while those in front are putting out. Then, the moment the green is free, they should be ready to have a practice swing and play the shot.

Quick players seldom back off the ball. They are far more decisive. Slow players, on the other hand, are apt to start hearing things and seeing things. By lingering, they are stretching their concentration to the limit.

Charlie Mechem thinks that teaching professionals are at least partly to blame for the way things have gone, in that they have instilled into their pupils the notion that they cannot operate without an elaborate pre-shot routine. As Charlie says, it all becomes faintly ridiculous when they bring this into play before a putt of no more than a couple of inches.

Charlie was not remotely upset when the USGA penalized two of his players to the tune of two shots apiece for slow play at The Broadmoor. (The US Open is run by the USGA rather than the LPGA.) He felt it backed up what he was trying to do on the tour.

We all know that there are big names on the men's circuits who have got away with murder on the slow-play front because of who they are, but Charlie, for one, was never afraid of pulling up the stars. Nancy Lopez and Jan Stephenson were both penalized during his term of office.

I was always of the opinion that fines for slow play were a complete waste of time. The perfect illustration, here, features David Leadbetter's wife, Kelly. In 1986, when she won the Hennessy tournament at Chantilly, Kelly was penalized to the tune of £50 for slow play in her third round. When tackled, she took a leaf from a famous Dave Hill story by suggesting that they ask for £100 because she was not going to be any quicker the next day. Since she was winning, and since the fine was only that, her husband had wisely counselled her against doing anything which might alter her rhythm. For Kelly, that £50 or £100 was money well spent.

Fines were replaced by two-stroke penalties, but they were seldom brought into play. In fact, no one was penalized on the WPGET tour in 1995, in spite of all the interminable rounds. With the penalty on such a big scale, the officials were reluctant to impose it without plenty in the way of evidence. Unfortunately, they were often too busy with other matters to collect the data.

The start of 1996 saw the introduction of the one-stroke penalty, which I think should provide the answer.* The WPGET explained over the winter that they were following the R&A's advice in toughening things up a bit. The onus, they said, would henceforth be on the players to keep up with the field rather than

---

* *Rule 6–7 Undue Delay. Slow Play*
  The player shall play without undue delay and in accordance with the pace of play guidelines which may be laid down by the Committee. Between completion of a hole and playing from the next teeing ground, the player shall not unduly delay play.
  PENALTY FOR BREACH OF RULE 6-7
  Match-play – Loss of hole; Stroke play – Two shots.
  For subsequent offence – Disqualification.
  Note 1: *If the player unduly delays play between holes, he is delaying the play of the next hole and the penalty applies to that hole.*
  Note 2: *For the purpose of preventing slow play, the Committee may, in the conditions of a competition, lay down pace of play guidelines including maximum periods of time allowed to complete a stipulated round, a hole or a stroke.*
  In stroke-play only, the Committee may, in such a condition, modify the penalty for a breach of this Rule as follows:
  First offence – One stroke
  Second offence – Two strokes
  For subsequent offence – Disqualification.

on the officials to keep urging them to hurry up. Now, if players fall behind, an official happening upon the golfing snails does not have to begin with any gentle chivvying. He can start timing them at once and impose a one-stroke penalty on the guilty party. If the same player offends for a second time, she will receive a two-stroke penalty. And if it happens for a third time in the course of a single round, she will be packing her bags and going home. The rules are in place, but I wonder if they will use them?

No one should pretend slow play is not a problem. Not when you think of the recent case of the amateur who, when asked why he was so slow, replied that people would think he wasn't trying if he didn't take his time. What on earth would someone like the late Cecil Leitch have made of that?

Back in the 1920s, this four-times winner of the Ladies' British Open Amateur Championship used to pride herself on getting round Silloth in one hour and 55 minutes. Let the great lady explain how it was done:

'We always had the same caddies who, like all good caddies, took the keenest interest in the game. They had only a few clubs to carry and, once putts had been holed, the club for the next tee shot was handed out and the caddies would then run forward to spot the balls and to be ready with the necessary club for the next shot.'

Chapter 10

Rules – for Better for Worse

There is no room in golf for what Greg Norman did to Mark McCumber at the tail end of last year in the NEC World Series of Golf at Firestone. Norman alleged that the American had cheated. To recap, there was a bug on McCumber's line and McCumber flicked it off. Norman said nothing at the time but he afterwards accused McCumber of having tapped down a spike mark. McCumber was adamant that that was not the case; that he had merely been removing the insect. (See relevant ruling below.)

In the absence of further evidence, the US PGA's senior Director of Rules, Mike Shea, said that since Norman's claims could not be substantiated, he would sign McCumber's card himself.

What I want to know is how Norman could be so certain about what he saw. I have sometimes seen things I thought amiss but, beyond maybe asking Matthew if he noticed anything, I would keep my mouth shut. I would tend to take the view that I had been seeing things, that the mistake was mine.

I would only steam in if it were something absolutely blatant which I had watched not just out of the corner of my eye but with both eyes working in conjunction with my full attention.

In the Norman-McCumber case, Norman was dealing with a very much wider issue than whether the bug was a spike-mark or vice versa. He was putting a man's good name in jeopardy. What he did was very disruptive. He upset not just McCumber but his entire family. When I played with McCumber in the JCPenney event last year, he was still mortified and desperate to talk. Who wouldn't be?

When the English Ladies' Golf Association had reports that two girls had been falsifying scores on the amateur tour a few years ago, they sent out a club official specifically to watch what was going on. The official in question kept her distance, but marked up the shots they were taking as they went along and then compared her findings with what was on the girls' cards. (The two players were banned for a three-year spell which was later reduced to two.) ELGA felt they had to be absolutely sure of their facts, and that is the way everyone else ought to think.

There is another consideration which comes into play, too, though it maybe sounds a little selfish. Obviously, you have no option but to get involved when you see a flagrant flouting of the rules. However, if you start accusing your playing companion of breaking the rules when you have no more than a niggling suspicion, you can say goodbye to your own golf for the day. There is no way you will be able to concentrate in such circumstances.

High handicappers who invoke the rules right, left and centre can also be the proverbial pain in the neck. I will never forget that ridiculous story of a third-team club match in the Midlands in which one of the visiting players quick-hooked her opening tee shot into the bushes. Her opponent, a homely creature who had been inveigled into the proceedings more for her ability to knock up a cake than a high wedge, involved herself in the search with characteristic zest. She found the ball and, in her excitement, picked it up and held it aloft.

The visitor's reaction was not quite what she had anticipated. 'Thank you, but now you have lifted it, I will have to claim the hole.'

In matches at that level, golfers would do better to stick to the spirit of the law rather than its letter. I know I would but, in fairness, I should perhaps explain that player and playing companion are not really allowed to agree to waive the rules. Take this illustration from the *Decisions on the Rules of Golf*:

Rule 1–3/4
Failure of players to apply known penalty.
Q. *In a match a player discovers at the 2nd hole that he has fifteen clubs in his bag contrary to Rule 4-4a but his opponent refuses to apply the penalty. The extra club is declared out of play and the match continues. The committee disqualifies both players. Is this correct?*
A. *Yes. Since the players agreed to waive the penalty, they should be disqualified under Rule 1–3.*

To be honest, no one has yet convinced me that the *Rules of Golf* add up to anything less than a joke. Sometimes, they will allow a golfer to get away with murder.

I got away with murder during my third round in the 1987 US Open win. I hit a wayward second at the 9th which finished 20–30 yards left of the green and under branches hanging so low that they barely cleared the turf. If I had had to play the ball as it lay, I would have been looking at a five at best. As luck would have it, a grandstand stood between that tree and the green and, to my amazement, an official appeared from nowhere and ushered me round to an inviting little dropping zone. I still had a relatively awkward shot, because I had to play to an elevated part of the green, but I was able to escape with the most improbable of fours.

On tour, the professionals are constantly looking for relief from rabbit scrapes and cart paths. If they are sufficiently hard-nosed to wait for the time it takes for an official to come along, they will often get what they want. Myself, I seldom wait, not just because I get agitated but because I can sense others around me getting that way. To give just one example, when I was defending my US Open title at Indianwood, my companions recommended I call for a ruling concerning the sprinkler head which was liable to interfere with my little shot to the 1st green. I waited and waited but when, after seven or eight minutes, the people behind were getting restless and there was still no sign of the officials' buggy approaching, I went ahead and played.

Heaven knows whether I would have got relief in that instance, but the shot I had to manufacture was one which left me with a nasty ten-footer which I missed. I started with a bogey, the last thing I wanted.

Although I know the experts say it is impossible, the *Rules of Golf* should be reduced to a three-page pamphlet which everyone can understand. And while they are about it, officialdom should alter the rules concerning Out of Bounds. Why should you have to hit three off the tee after launching one over the fence? Why isn't it two? That would be enough of a penalty. I am also entirely opposed to having Out of Bounds areas inside a golf course, unless it is in the interests of safety. Why penalize the player who is prepared to take the risks attached to cutting corners or playing one hole via another? The golfer should not find himself in trouble because of the shortcomings of the course's architect.

Now, back to spike marks.* Why on earth are you not allowed to poke them down? Once you are on the green, you should have as perfect a surface as possible. If, in a match-play situation, you have a five-footer over someone else's spike mark and your opponent has a five-footer over perfect pile, how on earth can that be deemed fair?

* *Rule 16–1*
a) Touching Line of Putt
The line of putt must not be touched except:
 i) the player may move sand and loose soil on the putting green and other loose impediments by picking them up or by brushing them aside with his hand or a club without pressing anything down;
 ii) in addressing the ball, the player may place the club in front of the ball without pressing anything down;
 iii) in measuring;
 iv) in lifting the ball;
 v) in pressing down a ball-marker;
 vi) in removing movable obstructions.
c) Repair of Hole Plugs, Ball Marks and Other Damage
The player may repair an old hole plug or damage to the putting green caused by the impact of a ball, whether or not the player's ball lies on the putting green. If the ball is moved in the process of repair, it shall be replaced, without penalty. Any other damage to the putting green shall not be repaired if it might assist the player in his subsequent play of the hole.

Chapter 11

A Round with Nicklaus and Daly

Years ago, when I teed up alongside Nancy Lopez for the first time on the LPGA tour, I remember feeling decidedly uneasy. I was anxious not to make a hash of things in front of the player who has always been one of my greatest heroines. On 12 September 1995, I felt much the same, only worse. I was due to play with Jack Nicklaus and John Daly in the Wendy's Three-Tour Challenge at Muirfield Village. As the title suggests, this is an event involving one player each from the three Amerian tours: the men's senior tour, the men's regular tour and the women's circuit. The top three players on the respective money lists are the first to be invited.

For weeks, everyone had been digging me in the ribs and saying, 'Bet you can't wait,' or something along those lines. In a way, I was itching for the big day but, when I woke up on the morning in question, I was feeling horribly sick.

Where John Daly was concerned, I did not know quite what to expect. I had long been a fan but, at the same time, I was more than a little fed up with being compared to someone who had a penchant for wrecking the odd hotel room and having fights in the car park. If I had any real picture of him at all, it was that he would be unutterably loud.

With Jack Nicklaus, on the hand, I knew the score. Here was a living legend. It would be dreadful to do badly in his company. Somehow, I had to prove that I deserved to be playing down the same fairways as the man who has won a total of 20 majors. What made it still more daunting was the fact that Muirfield Village is his own course and his own design. For obvious reasons, I did not want to be caught making any dumb tactical errors.

I was on the practice ground, rehearsing my opening lines as much as any of my shots, when Daly came across, hand outstretched. He introduced himself in the nicest possible way and, would you believe, we got on like a house on fire. So well, in fact, that at the end of the day he asked me if I would partner him in the JCPenney tournament. We have since fixed to play this year. (Last year, I played with Mark McCumber when David Feherty, my partner from 1994, was ineligible. Feherty lost his American card and was about to head into the world of American television commentary when he changed his mind and went back to his old stamping-ground, the PGA European Tour. There has been word of a new mixed event in Europe and, if that comes to pass, I would hope that David and I will get together again. He is endlessly humorous and a great playing companion.)

People were right all along in what they had been saying about John and me being alike. We are very similar. Apart from the obvious parallels on the big-hitting front, it soon became clear that we share much the same easy-going approach. Also, we both play at the same pace. I have always thought that my length has at least something to do with getting on the tee and hitting the ball at a time when I still have this incredible urge to hit it. John, it seems, is stirred by much the same feelings. He hates to hang around.

Far from being loud, he was one of the most shy and unassuming professionals I have ever met. He once or twice referred to his darker times by starting off a sentence with, 'In my drinking days,' but he did not speak much about himself. Except, that is, when I got him on to the subject of the Open.

I asked what he had felt like as he watched Costantino Rocca's putt going down at the 18th and he described it as 'a thump in the stomach', before adding that he had gone from holding the Claret

Jug 'in my mind' to suddenly having to work for it all over again.

He said he had been particularly touched at the way in which some of his fellow American professionals had come up to him before he set out on the play-off. Men like Brad Faxon, Tom Watson, Lorne Roberts and Payne Stewart had all sought him out and told him he could still win.

It does not need me to tell you that Jack Nicklaus is a wonderful man. A couple of years ago, we all heard that odd story about how Jack had played his part in dissuading the London Club from holding one of our women's tour events over the course he had designed there. He was said to have made it clear that he did not want the women messing about on it and that the London Club would do better to have a men's tournament instead.

Apparently, that was a massive misunderstanding. All he had said was that his course was not ready for any kind of tournament – professional or even amateur.

Allow me take you on to the 1st tee in a bid to convey what it was like having to hit off in the same party as these golfing gods. John hit first from the regular men's tees; Jack went second from the senior tees, and I went third from a tee a yard or so in front of Jack.

The two of them got great drives away. As I walked up to my teeing area, I admitted to Jack that I had never felt so nervous in all my life. 'You're having us on,' said Jack, lightly.

I hit a low, cutty shot into a fairway bunker. A horror. Mercifully, that was it. My next shot was a pretty miraculous affair, an improvised five iron from an awkward stance which headed straight for the green. It finished just over the back in another bunker, but it had at least demonstrated that I could play a bit. To my relief, I then got up and down for a par, and no pill could have done more to quell my nerves.

As we played, so it struck me that Jack had a huge respect for women golfers rather than the reverse. If he hadn't, he would never have involved himself in something like the Three-Tour Challenge.

There was not a lot of chat on the way round in that things were taken pretty seriously. For the record, John and I both had 73s while Jack was round in 72. In terms of length, Jack and I were about the same, with John ripping his tee shots 60 yards past ours. Mind you, I did hit a monster at the 18th which left me around 80 yards past what was, admittedly, not exactly one of Jack's greatest drives.

Jack was nice enough to say that while he had heard all about my long hitting, and that he had been taken aback by the strength of my short game. Indeed, when we came to the last hole, and I came up with what was one of my best chips of the day, he walked ahead and clapped me on to the putting surface. It was quite a moment.

For my part, I was surprised by John Daly's play around the greens. Several times, it looked as if he were 'dead', but each time he emerged to within a couple of inches of the hole. In particular, there was a shot from the right-hand greenside bunker at the short 8th. I can see it now. His ball was buried under the front lip and, as I passed by, I had thought to myself, 'Impossible.'

He not only got it out but put spin on it, leaving himself not much more than a tap-in.

When I expressed amazement to Jack, his reply interested me more than somewhat. 'You would never have heard of John Daly if he didn't have a good short game. There are plenty of others who can hit the ball as far as he can but who haven't even made the tour.'

The seniors came out on top in each of their three games, their performance bearing out what Gary Player has been saying recently about the latest equipment having narrowed the gap between the men's regular tour and the seniors.

When the golf clubs were packed away, Jack Nicklaus invited us back to a tea party hosted by his wife, Barbara, at their holiday home on the edge of the course. Kelly Robbins was there, as was Dottie Pepper, who is managed by Jack Nicklaus's Golden Bear Organization and who, I have to say, is perfectly friendly in an off-course context! Lee Trevino and Hale Irwin were the male guests.

As we tucked into a wonderful spread, I was very conscious of the fact that the day had been the stuff of most golfing folk's dreams, not least my own.

There is, of course, a lesson in all this. One of the best things about the game of golf is that its format, with the handicap system and the different teeing areas, allows for good players and not-so-good to play side by side.

While I think I can perhaps be forgiven for having been alarmed at the prospect of playing with John Daly and Jack Nicklaus, it is not uncommon for a club golfer to feel beaten by the supposedly better player even before he or she hits from the first tee.

I remember a women's Woolmark Match-Play championship in which Lora Fairclough beat Marie-Laure de Lorenzi in a year when Marie-Laure had just won eight tournaments and Lora was new on the scene. A lot of players might have run Marie-Laure close that day, but not too many would have had the belief it takes to seal the win. Lora had that belief, and I remember thinking, even then, that she was one to watch. A couple of years later, she was in the Solheim Cup side and playing magnificently.

No one, at any level, should ever take to the course feeling inferior to an opponent. Especially on the club scene, the system has taken care of that side of things. You are what you are – and if, for argument's sake, that is a 12 handicapper, you should not feel ashamed of it. You might learn something from rubbing shoulders with a better player, but the most important thing is that you should get out there and play your own game.

Chapter 12

Golf's New Strongholds

JAPAN

It was towards the end of 1995 that I started thinking in terms of spending a full season on the Japanese LPGA tour before the start of the next century. I have always been loyal to the European tour, which is currently sponsored by American Express, and I have done what I can to support Terry Coates, our Chief Executive, and those who were in office before him. But there are others I should think about as well, notably my endlessly helpful Japanese sponsors, Maruman. Over the years, they have become firm friends as much as sponsors.

My contract with the company goes back a long way, although at one time it played second fiddle to the arrangement I had with the Weetabix organization. The two combined well enough but, towards the end of a 1990 season which had not been one of my better golfing years, I 'fell out' with Weetabix over what happened at the AGF Biarritz Open.

The Biarritz tournament was usually a gem but, that year, it was a grimly rain-lashed affair which ended up being cut from four rounds to two. Even at that, I was mighty gratified to win. Up until then, I had failed to achieve the goal I had set myself on turning professional – of winning at least one tournament a year.

With everything in such disarray at the golf course – the clubhouse was packed with sodden souls who had come in to dry off and have a drink – it was decided that the prize-giving would be rather more of an occasion if it took place at the Palace Hotel down in the town. The photographers, in turn, decided that they would do better to take my picture in hotel surroundings. All of which explains how it came about that I appeared in *Golf Weekly* a few days later in ordinary clothing rather than golf gear bearing the Weetabix logo that I was paid to wear.

Because of this omission, Sir Richard George, the Chief Executive of the Weetabix organization, decided against paying the £8,000 bonus to which I would otherwise have been entitled. That, coupled with the fact that Sir Richard felt that my performances that year had not been in keeping with my talent, led to the split, though it has to be said that we never really fell out on a personal level. After all, I certainly could have no complaints, for Weetabix had paid me around $200,000 over a three-year stretch.

At the time, when I was asked by the press to answer Sir Richard's comments about my disappointing performances, I left it at this: 'I would love to have been "great" in Weetabix's eyes and to have lived up to their expectations, but I can only do my best, and I have never done anything less.'*

In November of that year, I was in a taxi with some of the Maruman people when I asked, out of the blue, if they would

---

* LM: Sir Richard George recalls that he had decided to end Laura's contract, together with those of his two other players, Muffin Spencer-Devlin and Sally Little, long before the Biarritz week . . .

'Obviously, what happened at Biarritz caused some argument. Our people who looked at the pictures after Laura's win and saw no Weetabix logo on her shirt, wondered what on earth we got out of the arrangement. (Unlike the other girls, Laura was not using a Weetabix golf bag.) They had a valid point. We did not want to pay the bonus, but, in a roundabout way, we paid it anyhow.

'Among the tournaments Laura won when she was with us was America's Jamie Farr Classic. We duly paid the agreed $12,500 bonus on that one, but when, some months later, the International Management Group invoiced us for a bonus for her win in Toledo, we paid up consider an overall sponsorship, one which would take in clothing as well as clubs. They agreed, and by the following March a deal was in place from which I have never looked back. The Maruman clubs are absolutely right for me, while the clothes, too, have been a great success.

From the first time I went to Japan, I felt very much at home there. My impression, like my mother's, was that it is a thoroughly pleasant and polite golfing land. Also, it is very different from the rest of Asia, an area which still produces a host of quaint golfing tales. I am thinking, in particular, of what happened at an event on the Asian PGA's new Omega Tour in Korea last year. Not wanting to spoil the practice putting green with holes, the club in question asked the professionals to putt through hoops. From Pakistan, on

again. Those dealing with the payments had failed to appreciate that the Jamie Farr and the Toledo event are one and the same thing.

'In the end, we came to an arrangement with IMG whereby we got out of the contract a month early and the two payments for the one tournament stood.

'My sums tally with Laura's; she was paid around $200,000 over a three-year stint.

'There were a couple of reasons why I had already come to the conclusion that these individual sponsorships were not the best idea from our point of view. Unlike our Weetabix British Women's Open championship, which is all to do with the UK, Laura was often playing in countries where we only sell a handful of Weetabix. That did not make sense.

'Also, I had already been looking into the business of getting more involved in The Prince's Trust. It occurred to me that whereas our individual golf sponsorships were not making any significant difference to the players' lifestyles in that they all had plenty of money already, the same amount donated to The Prince's Trust would make a huge difference to a whole lot of young people; people who really needed a helping hand. Since 1990, we have given the charity two million pounds.

'Having said all this, I would hate anyone to think that I am anything less than a Laura supporter. I am sure we benefited as much as she did in the early period of our sponsorship. She's a remarkable lady who has done wonders for the women's game.'

that same circuit, came the lovely tale of how Ricky Tilling, who was in charge of the Star TV coverage, was left to man the cameras himself on the second day as his Pakistani cameramen disappeared to observe a religious festival.

At first I was not too taken with the Japanese courses. It seemed that they were all built on the sides of mountains, and that almost every shot had to be played with one foot higher than the other. Also, there was far too much in the way of out-of-bounds for my liking. The more modern, American-type courses, on the other hand, suit me rather better. Even these have escalators up to the more elevated tees, but they are mostly a good deal flatter.

As the courses have improved, so have the players. Years ago, any mention of a Japanese woman golfer would connote pictures of neat and petite little golfers who were wholly inscrutable. On the question of size, the late Henry Longhurst once had a rude shock while commentating on a Colgate European Open of the early 1970s. He had kept referring to Chako Higuchi, of the famously swaying swing, as 'a tiny little girl', but when, eventually, he came face to face with the player, he discovered that, at five foot ten inches, she could look him squarely in the eye.

In terms of temperament, I myself always used to be under the illusion that the Japanese players were mentally impregnable, but I soon discovered that even the best of them could perform the extraordinary double of looking calm and having a mammoth blow-out at the one time. Most memorably, it happened to Ayako Okamoto at Plainfield in 1987, the year that she, JoAnne Carner and I ended up in that play-off for the US Open which I was lucky enough to win.

In the last round, Ayako had four putts on the 9th green. Then, at the 13th, she had three putts from two and a half feet. She solemnly putted one way and then another before leaving the green more in a trance than a temper.

For as long as I live, I will never forget the first tournament I played in Japan, the Konica Ladies' Open in 1987. It was on the third hole that my playing companion had one duff, followed by another and then another. I was standing quietly by, trying to convey that she should take her time, when, all of a sudden, I thought I heard laughter from behind the ropes. I looked up, alarmed.

The spectators were laughing, and it seemed to be infectious, spreading from one little group to the next. However, the tone of their laughter was not unkind. It was the absurdity of the situation which had got to them. They could not believe that such terrible things should be happening to so good a player.

Since that day, I have noticed that Japanese spectators only have to see a huge hook, a big slice or anything extreme, and they're practically rolling down the banks. Strange though it is, I have to say I have come to savour such Eastern idiosyncrasies.

It is going to be difficult when the time finally comes for me to make up my mind about whether to go along with Maruman's wishes and play there for a year. After all, my friends are mostly drawn from those who, like myself, switch from the European tour to the American circuit. However, if the the money is right (I don't mind admitting that that will help to influence me one way or the other), I will forget everything except for the American majors and the Weetabix British Women's Open and dedicate myself completely to the task in hand. Having said all that, I must point out that I would first have to go through the same maze of a qualifying school as anyone else. From what I have heard, it is a far more complex affair than in Europe and the States.

Though everyone says I am as street-wise in Japan as I am anywhere else in the world, my mastery of the Japanese language does not extend much beyond 'Good morning' and 'Thank you'. However, with my clubs doing the talking in between, that vocabulary, as one of the journalists joked, was entirely adequate for my trip to the 1994 Itoen Ladies tournament at Chonanmachi.

On that occasion, I turned up and won the first prize of 10.8 million yen ($108,000), together with the statutory car that goes with a winner's cheque. On top of that, there were three ornate trophies; a cash bonus from one of the joint sponsors, which was then outdone by one from another; a year's supply of tea; enough bales of rice to last me well into the next century, and a diamond necklace and matching bracelet.

The 1995 version, where I successfully defended my title, was equally lucrative. The haul included another $108,000 winner's purse, a Mazda limousine and a necklace dripping with diamonds.

Even if the language barrier prevents me from being particularly close to any of them, I feel entirely comfortable in the company of the Japanese women professionals. As often as not, I will join them for lunch at the end of a round – something which is altogether different to what would happen in America, where everyone is apt to go her own way. With an IMG aide acting as an interpreter, I can enjoy sharing in the happy small talk that is so much a part of the Japanese scene.

Akiko Fukishama, who like myself uses Maruman clubs, is the player with whom I probably have the most contact. The two of us often go together to sponsors' days, which can involve playing with Maruman clients or giving shows at a multi-storey driving range like the one at Shiba Park in Tokyo. There, you get a never-ending stream of golfers hitting from three levels. Some never graduate beyond the range, simply because it can cost anything up to £250,000 to join a club, with the subsequent annual subscription in much the same bracket.

On one occasion, Akiko and I went to a city store and hit shots into a large net. A computer had been installed to register how far we were hitting and in what direction. After we had unleashed a dozen or so balls apiece, shoppers were invited into the teeing area to see if they could do better. They enjoyed themselves hugely, and went into paroxysms of laughter as they swung themselves off their feet.

The people are very good to me, but Akiko, who is one of their own, is treated like a pop star or Princess Di. The daughter of a household name (a Japanese household, that is) in the realm of baseball, Akiko has her own range of clothing and her own line in jewellery.

You may not feel up to mastering many Japanese names, but hers is definitely worth the effort. She is still a teenager but she is already a great golfer. She is long, too . . . very long. I've hit a few big drives and, to my surprise, she's been right up there. Not all the time, but often enough.

Further to illustrate the high esteem in which the Japanese women golfers are held, let me tell you what happened when Ayako Okamoto got hit on the forehead by one of her pro-am partners on the eve of the Mazda Japan Classic.

To the sponsors' concern, the hospital kept her in for observation, and throughout the night a television crew and a crowd of reporters and photographers kept vigil at the door in the hope of snatching a word or a picture. They stayed throughout the next day and were still in position long after Ayako had escaped via a back door.

Okamoto and Fukishama giggle, politely, at all the attention they receive. Neither of them behaves like a prima donna, nor would any of the rest of the players on the Japanese circuit. No one would dream of walking past press or public and giving them the cold shoulder. If they did, the sponsors would not want them back. In Japan, you must treat everyone with respect, especially if you are a foreigner.

Company apart, I could always tell I was playing in Japan by the turf. The blades of grass are thick, but their roots almost non-existent. Take a divot and you get a scattering of sand. I find clubbing difficult, though I have no doubt that it would come more easily were I there for a long stint.

Another clue as to where I was would be provided by the fastidious manicuring which goes on at all of the better Japanese courses. There are American courses which, with their assorted blooms, are as colour film against black-and-white, but in Japan the effect can sometimes be that of a perfectly groomed garden. As Peter Dobereiner related in his *Glorious World of Golf*, 'There are gardens with trim beds of chrysanthemums bordering the tees, trees painstakingly cultured into satisfying shapes, and crystal-clear water hazards floored with hand-picked stones and stocked with ornamental fish and flowering plants . . . It is a positive pleasure to slice into a Japanese pond.'

The amount of land devoted to the game is mirrored in the amount of space given to it in the daily papers. Even if there are only a couple of Japanese girls teeing up in a major American event like the Dinah Shore, as many as a dozen Japanese journalists and photographers will fly over to watch. In these circumstances, they will stick with their own players through thick and thin, the other competitors seeming to hold very little interest. Nor is the sport ignored on Japanese television. On the occasion of that US Open play-off, the live coverage being beamed back to Japan apparently drew the second largest television audience for any golf tournament anywhere in the world, the largest having been the British Open.

Though American professionals, on their annual end-of-season visit to Japan, are apt to take their own packets of breakfast cereal with them, I am a little different in that I genuinely like Japanese food. My only concession to my Western upbringing is to have a jar of Marmite in my baggage. Curious locals, looking for reasons behind my length, are under the impression that it is a species of magic tar.

At home there are a couple of Japanese fans – not, as someone noted, the human variety – leaning up against the windows of my house. Also, a little Sumo wrestler has pride of place on a table in the lounge.

I think I would be tempted to put him away if Terry Coates, the Executive Director of the Women's European Tour, were coming to tea. Terry would clearly prefer it if I were not thinking about going over there. However, I think he will understand if I do decide to hit out in this very different direction. After all, a single season is soon gone.

SWEDEN

We are sometimes very slow to face facts in this country. Like a second coming of the Vikings, the Swedes are taking over in golf and it is about time that people sat up and took notice.

Lotta Neumann, Helen Alfredsson and Annika Sorenstam have

won four majors in the last eight years, while the number of Swedes in the Solheim Cup matches played to date has gone up as follows: two in 1990; three in 1992; four in 1994. Lotta won the 1996 Tournament of Champions in the States by a massive 11 shots, and she and Annika were both in the top three on the Ping World Leaderboard at the turn of last year.

Now look at the way in which Swedish club golfers have multiplied. In the early 1900s, fewer than 100 people played golf in Sweden. By 1955, their number was up to 7,000, these divided over 39 courses. 'Then,' as Tom Callahan wrote in *Golf Digest* in 1994, 'an ice hockey star named Sven Tumba took up the game and overnight the golfing population doubled, tripled and quadrupled. Today, of the eight million Swedes sprinkled the length of the country, 320,000 call themselves golfers and more than 300 clubs are straining at the seams.'

When Tumba, as Callahan explained, was through with the Olympic Games, the Swedish National Soccer Team and the US National Hockey League, he brought Sam Snead, Arnold Palmer and Jack Nicklaus to his homeland for golf exhibitions which whetted the national appetite.

To me, though, it seems that it all started when the then 15-year-old Lotta Neumann came from nowhere to win the Swedish Women's Amateur Stroke-Play championship in 1981. She had been on one of the junior squads which had popped up all over the land, but she had never previously teed up in a senior event. Her compatriots in that championship had never heard of the girl from Finspang. Not only that, but they did not even know there was a golf course in that neck of the woods. If memory serves me aright, Lotta won by a mile.

That same summer, Sweden leapt to the fore in European golfing circles when they picked up both the European Senior and Junior Team championships. Here in Britain, we should have responded by redoubling our efforts. Instead, we wasted a lot of time refusing to believe what we were seeing and making jokes about things such as the physical jerks the Swedes did first thing each morning during the junior event at Wentworth. Also, we did our best to shrug off their efforts by making out that they were not always adhering to the rules of amateur status.

In 1983, England had the better of Sweden in the final of the European Junior Team championship in Holland – an occasion which has meant more with the passing of years in that I defeated Lotta in the last day's singles. However, the Swedes grabbed the title back in 1984, and it was in 1987, when they captured the European Senior Team championship for a second time, that our officials at last acknowledged that they were guilty of nothing more sinister than bringing an admirably professional approach to amateur golf.

One thing everyone was beginning to notice around that time was that whereas some of our teenagers tended to be a little bit blasé about the overseas trips they were getting, the Swedes were approaching every tournament and practice session with a wide-eyed enthusiasm.

I have often discussed these developments with my Scandinavian friends on tour. It seems that the overriding concern of their officials is that young Swedes should enjoy their golf. They have golfing holiday camps where, as Jesper Parnevik was remembering recently, every child leaves with a bagful of sweets, chocolates and golf balls – and longs to return.

Annika, when asked about her junior days, likened the Swedish network to the most homely of spiderwebs: 'You only had to reach out a little way and someone would help you.'

Pia Nilsson, the Director of Swedish Golf, believes that if young golfers are to go on enjoying the game, they must always be treated consistently. She abhors the kind of situation in which a youngster is in favour one minute and out of favour the next. If, for instance, an amateur who has represented Sweden had to be dropped from the national team to make room for someone who was hitting the ball better, Pia would be on the phone to the player to give her a full explanation as to how the selectors' minds had worked. She would also advise on what the girl would have to do to get back into the side.

I can guarantee that if Pia Nilsson had been in charge, there would have been no 'Sue Lovatt incident' at last year's Home

Internationals in Wrexham. The Welsh golfer 'did a runner' on the first day after she had been left out of both the foursomes and the singles. Maureen Madill, who is Wales's official coach, eventually traced her to her home and told her to come back, not least because she was due to play alongside Vicki Thomas against England the next morning. The player did not want to know.

Though there was some confusion over the wording of their announcement, the Welsh Ladies' Golf Union decreed that Sue Lovatt would never represent her country again. They further ordained that she could not enter any tournament run under the umbrella of the WLGU for ten years – in other words, until she was 45. An amazingly severe punishment, unless, of course, she robbed a bank on her way home.

Sue Lovatt should never have done what she did, but why on earth did someone not keep her abreast of developments? The fact that she was asked to go out and practise while her team-mates were playing their foursomes must have led her to think she would be needed for the singles. But when lunch came and the singles line-up was given out, she did not get a mention. Nor, reportedly, did anyone look her in the eye. Surely, someone should have found the guts and the time to have a quiet word with her before the singles players were named?

As it was, she spent the afternoon feeling totally rejected, with her mind turning to things which had gone wrong in the past. As a youngster, she apparently felt that she had been made to suffer for choosing to be coached by her grandfather instead of one of the teachers recognized by the Welsh Ladies' Golf Union.

Returning to the Swedish set-up, there is a deal of emphasis placed on a 'team' approach. Indeed, not long ago Chris Hodenfield hazarded in an American magazine that the Swedes heard more about the ideals of harmony and teamwork than would the work-force in a Japanese transmission factory. It is this which contributes to the way in which any group of Swedes at a professional tourna-ment will be buzzing with positive vibes. They will often dine out together, especially when Pia is around. She quite understands if they do not want to go, but the invitation is always there for those who want the company. (As one who turned professional back in 1981, at a time when there were no other Swedes on tour, Pia knows about loneliness. When she moved into the realm of administration, she vowed that the Swedes who followed in her wake would benefit from a first-class support system.)

What greatly helps with the implementation of this caring approach at every level is that there is only the one body, the Swedish Federation. This organization is in charge of amateurs and professionals, juniors and seniors, men and women.

In Britain, by contrast, there is a huge divide between the women's amateur bodies and the professional tour, even though the Ladies' Golf Union and the American Express European Tour have attempted to forge links.

As a British amateur, you play your golf for either the English, Scottish, Welsh or Irish association and for the Ladies' Golf Union. You try your guts out for them in junior and senior international matches and, generally speaking, you put up with any erratic happenings on the team selection front simply because it is not in your interests to fall out with the people at the helm.

Things may be rather better now, but in my day, when you decided to turn professional, that was the end of you as far as the LGU were concerned. You were 'scum'. They would then concentrate on the next generation, who got the same treatment in their turn when they left the amateur game.

Newcomers can have a very hard time of it on the professional tour. Cut off from the amateur network and suddenly left to do everything for themselves, they encounter all sorts of awkward situations. If, in turning professional, they have been lent some cash, they will be under pressure to pay it back; if they have found a sponsor, they will be desperate to prove they were worth sponsoring.

I remember one British girl who received financial help from a firm of seed merchants who, it seemed, expected much the same results from their player as they did from a packet of their own produce. They kept ringing for reports on her progress and, almost inevitably, there was none.

Pia Nilsson uses a gardening analogy where her players are concerned. She does not expect the careers of all of her charges to proceed at any given rate, appreciating, as she does, that some will flower almost too soon and then take time to re-establish themselves; and that others could be out there for several seasons before finally blooming.

Even when a Swede makes it to the very top, she will not be ignored. Pia pays regular visits to both the European and American tours and if, say, Annika or any of the others wants a bit of help on the practice ground, Pia will be only too happy to help. She will do a lot of watching during a tournament and, from time to time, she will take notes on a girl's course management or how she comes across from a spectator's point of view. Is she playing at a reasonable pace? Does she look happy about her business? After a round, she might follow the player concerned into the press room and see how she handles her press conference. The Swedes don't miss a trick.

Swedish temperaments interest me more than somewhat. Lotta and Annika are wonderfully calm. They might get a touch ruffled when something goes wrong, but they always have everything back together long before they are due to play their next shot. When it comes to Helen Alfredsson, Catrin Nilsmark and Carin Hjalmarson, all of them, especially Alfie, can go mad but without making a habit of it. Alfie, for instance, more or less blew the US Open at Indianwood in 1994 but was sufficiently strong, mentally, to come back and win the following week.

In terms of the golf they play, most of the Swedes – Alfie is the exception here – are 'down the middle merchants'. Thanks not least to their wide-ranging training, they plot their way round the course as well as anyone on tour.

Over the winter, some or all of the top players will look in on the odd Swedish training camp, mostly as a means of putting something back into a system which has served them so well. I don't need to spell out to you what it must do for Sweden's up-and-coming youngsters when they can rule shoulders with a player like Annika, fresh from winning the US Open.

Chapter 13

The Solheim Cup

It all happened very fast. In the mid 1980s, when John Laupheimer was in power on America's LPGA tour, any suggestion of a Ryder Cup type of match between the American women and ourselves was politely dismissed. Laupheimer and Co. made it abundantly clear that the Europeans were light years away from being ready for such a fixture. To be fair, they could be forgiven for thinking as much. The Americans, after all, had the benefit of playing week in, week out, in a relentlessly tough school and for a lot of money besides. We, on the other hand, were playing on a European tour which was still in its formative years.

My win in the 1987 US Open did something to narrow the gulf in their eyes, and when Lotta Neumann won the following year's US Open, the scene was set for Joe Flanagan, our own Executive Director and a man who deserved an infinitely better chit from the women than he ever got, to start discussing things for real.

With the Ping organization having the necessary vision to come in as sponsors, the first match was set for 16–18 November at Lake Nona, David Leadbetter's Florida base.

The first question to exercise the pundits' minds concerned the title of the match. There was a trophy, the Babe Zaharias, which was being played for intermittently on the Scottish amateur circuit. The Babe, as is well known, was arguably the greatest golfer of all time, a natural athlete who won two gold medals in the 1932 Olympics before switching to golf. In 1946 and 1947 she won 15 amateur tournaments in a row, including the US Amateur and the British. As a professional, she won three US Opens and ten majors overall. She was also the John Daly of her day. Apparently, when she played at Muirfield during the week that she was in Scotland for the British Open at Gullane, she never needed more than an eight iron for any second shot. There are old hands at Muirfield who remember it well.

As many in the golfing fraternity started pressing for that title, so Elaine Farquharson, the Scottish amateur who held the Babe Zaharias Trophy at that time, was told not to let it out of her sight. Those to whom The Babe's husband had entrusted the cup had no intention of having it removed from the Scottish scene.

They need not have bothered to go to such lengths. In the interim, another name had been agreed. The match would be called the Solheim Cup, in honour of Karsten Solheim, the founder of the Ping empire and a man whose brand-name putters are wielded to good effect all around the golfing globe.

No one expected the Solheim Cup automatically to take its place alongside such established events as the Ryder, Walker and Curtis Cups. After all, these three were steeped in years of tradition. Yet, extraordinary though it may seem, the Solheim Cup slotted into that exclusive company at the first time of asking. The Ping people could not have given their match a more prestigious start. Far from doing things on the cheap, they had thought of everything. One glittering social occasion followed another on the days leading up to the match, while Lake Nona was the perfect choice for an event finding its feet. This being the first year, there was never going to be an endless stream of spectators pouring through the gates. But those who came were mostly connoisseurs, keen golfers who appreciated that the European professionals were a relatively new breed and therefore up against it from the start.

Our relative strengths can be illustrated by the players' collective records. The Americans, among them, had 16 majors under their belts. We, on the other hand, had only two – Lotta's US Open title and mine.

· I think it is fair to say that our own supporters homed in on Lake Nona with their fingers crossed. To be perfectly honest, they weren't really thinking of a European win but just praying devoutly that we would succeed in making a match of it. The players felt more confident of giving the Americans a run for their money but, at the back of our minds, I suppose that we knew that our first priority was to avoid the whitewash which Betsy King had apparently predicted for us. Such an outcome would set the European cause back years. It would be in keeping with that Hitachi British Women's Open held at Woburn in 1984 and won by Ayako Okamoto. Ayako looked a class apart as she won by miles from a field struggling from back tees and in bad conditions. The BBC, who had tried to give live coverage of this demoralizing spectacle, described it as a total disaster from their point of view. They said a lot of things would need to happen before they came back.

The 1990 European Solheim Cup side met in a London hotel before travelling to Lake Nona. The excitement was out of this world – partly nervousness and partly the sheer thrill of being involved in the first match in the series. The Americans, on the other hand, would probably be the first to admit that they were far from being as caught up in the proceedings as they are today. Certainly, the inaugural match did not feature in their everyday conversation as it did in ours. As the event drew closer, however, it became evident that none of the better American players wanted to miss out.

Ali Nicholas and I were paired together in practice over a course which we loved from the start. It was wooded, yet there was plenty of room; it was dotted with water hazards, but none of them was ridiculously intrusive. The greens were severely undulating and, as Michael Williams predicted in *The Daily Telegraph*, the Americans would always be more comfortable on them than we were.

When it came to the first foursomes series, Mickey Walker, who at St Pierre will be captaining the side for a fourth time, put Ali and myself out top. Ali can remember our nervous wait on the tee. Having compared notes on how awful we were both feeling, I apparently turned to her and observed, 'Here's someone coming who's not going to make you feel any better.'

It was Nancy Lopez. This winner of 47 tour titles was playing alongside Pat Bradley, who is equally awe-inspiring in her own way.

What gave us a good feeling from the start was that the crowd did not seem to see us as the enemy. I suppose they thought that we looked rather an unlikely couple, what with my being so big and Ali so tiny. 'A cute couple' is what they called us.

The 1st was halved, but we went ahead at the long 2nd when Ali hit our third, a long bunker shot, to within three feet. We made a birdie to take the lead and, though Nancy holed from 20 feet to draw level at the 8th, we went ahead again with a birdie at the 12th. The Americans more or less presented us with the 14th and that, in turn, furnished us with the confidence we needed to finish them off, with the score 2 and 1.

Nancy was endlessly gracious in defeat. In fact, what she said when the match was done undoubtedly encouraged Ali to have another crack at the LPGA tour, her first attempt having been wracked by homesickness. 'You could definitely make it out here,' is what Nancy said to her. She was right enough. At the time of writing, Ali has already won twice in the States.

One of the reasons those words meant so much is that Ali, like me, was reared on tales of the charismatic Nancy Lopez. As a teenager, she had been given a copy of Nancy's first book and spent hours wondering if she would ever get to play alongside the New Mexican.

Kathy Whitworth, in her analysis of that top match, wondered if she had been right to pair Lopez with Bradley. Her thinking was that they were the Americans' most seasoned players and that they would rejoice in leading the way. Afterwards, she felt that the combination of her two 'megastars' had been a mistake. Ali and I, she suggested, had been fired up as we would never have been against a less celebrated couple.

Alas, we did not win another point on the first day. Most of those spectators who were able to flit from match to match commented on how the Americans started making great putts from the 1st hole, whereas for a long time the Europeans had the look of players trying desperately to get the feel of the greens. Yet the mere fact that we had one match in the bag was a relief. There was not going to be any whitewash.

In the following day's fourballs, we lost three matches in a row before Lotta and Pam Wright combined magnificently to defeat Cathy Gerring and Dottie Mochrie on the 16th green. Gerring, incidentally, was a great little player who had to drop out of golf the following year after her hands and face were badly burned in an accident at a tented village on one of the tournament sites. She had gone to get the hot dish of the day when flames leapt from the gas ring below, engulfing her face and hands. Her face did not take long to recover, but her hands were so badly affected that she had no hope of gripping a golf club. Sad though it was that her burgeoning career should have been interrupted in such a terrible way, she took it magnificently insisting that she was lucky the accident had been no worse.

With two days gone, we were trailing 6–2. Eight singles lay ahead on the Sunday, and Mickey Walker, an outstanding captain in every way, could not have prepared us better in the circumstances.

The first match, between Cathy Gerring and Helen Alfresson, was one in which the American always had the upper hand in winning by 4 and 3. The next was between me and Rosie Jones. I have to admit that I was a shade disappointed when I heard I had got Rosie Jones. It is not that I don't admire her as a player, it was simply that I wanted to get my hands on a Patty Sheehan or a Beth Daniel – one of the 'in' players of the moment.

Mind you, all that changed with something Rosie said at the first hole. It may have been inadvertent, but she suddenly imbued me with the feeling that there was no one I wanted to beat more than Rosie Jones.

I had hit a two iron from the tee and, as we started off down the fairway, she turned to me and asked, 'Is there a screw loose in your driver or something?'

She was perhaps only introducing the kind of light-hearted banter that can be part and parcel of match-play, but in this context it left me more irritated than amused. Mercifully, I had the presence of mind to retort, good-naturedly, than I didn't need my driver – and won by 3 and 2.

After that, we had three points in the bag. Dale Reid, who comes from Ladybank in Scotland, would come up with another, her victim none other than Patty Sheehan. Dale started with four birdies in the first six holes and was unstoppable thereafter against an opponent who, that year alone, had won five times on the American tour and finished second on their money list.

The other European to evade defeat on that last afternoon was Pam Wright, whose Scottish home is farther north than Dale's – Aboyne, to be precise. She finished with a half against Betsy King which should have been a win. Why the golfing Gods should have decreed otherwise I cannot think. The match was all square, and Pam was on the green of the 18th in two, when King hit her second towards Lake Nona. There were only a handful of trees on the lake's edge, all of them pretty skeletal affairs. But, would you believe, Betsy's ball hit a branch and from there ricocheted on to the front of the putting surface. Betsy herself was stunned, taking an age to swallow that bit of luck. Then, when she got herself together, she almost holed her putt for a three. That, though, would have been just too much to take. They halved the hole, and small wonder that Pam went straight to her mum, who, having been a Curtis Cup golfer herself, understood only too well what her daughter was going through.

The overall scoreline was a disappointing 11½–4½. Had there been any justice at all, it would have been better, but, as Mickey Walker said, each point or half point on the board had represented a monumental achievement, and not least because of what Betsy had said about the Americans not losing a match.

Points apart, Kathy Whitworth, the American captain, sent us away with some very encouraging words. Like Walker, she felt we had acquitted ourselves well, and she said that she could see for herself how the gap in standard between the USA and Europe was narrowing. The next encounter, she predicted, might be a deal closer.

1st Solheim Cup 16–18 November 1990 Lake Nona, Florida, USA.

Foursomes
L Daves and A Nicholas beat P Bradley and N Lopez 2 & 1
P Wright and L Neuman lost to C Gerring and D Mochrie 6 & 5
D Reid and H Alfredsson lost to P Sheehan and R Jones 6 & 5
T Johnson and M L de Lorenzi lost to B Daniel and B King 5 & 4
Foursomes: EUROPE 1, USA 3

Fourballs
T Johnson and M L de Lorenzi lost to P Sheehan and R Jones 2 & 1
D Reid and H Alfredsson lost to P Bradley and N Lopez 2 & 1
L Davies and A Nicholas lost to B King and B Daniel 4 & 3
L Neumann and P Wright beat C Gerring and D Mochrie 4 and 2
Fourballs: EUROPE 1, USA 3

Singles
H Alfredsson lost to C Gerring 4 & 3
L Davies beat R Jones 3 & 2
A Nicholas lost to N Lopez 6 and 4
P Wright halved with B King
L Neumann lost to B Daniel 7 & 6
D Reid beat P Sheehan 2 & 1
M L de Lorenzi lost to D Mochrie 4 & 2
T Johnson lost to P Bradley 8 & 7
Singles: EUROPE 2½, USA 5½

FINAL SCORE: USA 11½, EUROPE 4½

One of my abiding memories of the second Solheim Cup – at Dalmahoy in October 1992 – is of Ali calling to me from across the car park in front of the hotel.

'We've got them!' is what she said. She was referring to the fact that we would be teeing up the next morning against Betsy King and Beth Daniel in the first foursome. Her excitement probably had less to do with the fact that we had lost to the two of them in the fourballs at Lake Nona two years earlier than with what Beth had said in a magazine interview which appeared by way of a preview to Dalmahoy.

The relevant remark?

'You could put any of us (Americans) in the European side and make it better.'

Beth, a golfer who has always called a spade a spade, would strongly deny that she had said any such thing. Maybe not, but the writer in question was the greatly respected Geoff Russell, a man who is well known for telling things as they are. Consequently, no one was in too much of a hurry to take her side.

As you may remember, the British tabloids had a field day with the Daniel comment. It was just what they wanted in order to bring the match to life. By the time they had quizzed the Europeans and their captain for their views, the atmosphere could scarcely have been more electric.

Nor was that the only thing to go wrong for the Americans in the days leading up to the match. Sadly, Kathy Whitworth, who had captained her troops so well at Lake Nona and was set to fulfil the same role at Dalmahoy, had to return home to tend her dying mother. Alice Miller, the President of the LPGA, would take her place but, though it was hardly her fault, the golfers did not have the same relationship with her as they had with Kathy. The latter's 81 wins on the LPGA tour were in themselves enough to keep the American Solheim Cup superstars in line.

On a very wet Friday morning, Ali and I opened with a couple of birdies to win the first two holes against Betsy and Beth. Mickey was able to relay the good news to those of our team-mates who were just teeing off at the 1st. We followed those two birdies with a run of bogey, par, bogey, par before finishing off the first nine with two more birdies. By then two up, we went three ahead at the 10th where Ali knocked a four wood just inches from the flag and Betsy's second, from the right rough, failed to reach the green after tangling in mid-air with what looked like a bird's nest.

We were feeling pretty pleased with ourselves and they were already in bad humour when Beth asked for the green at the 11th to be squeegeed before she played her chip. David Parkin, the referee who is now working on the up-and-coming new Asian PGA circuit, explained that the green had been mopped before they played their second shots and that the policy which had been agreed was that it could only be done the once.

The Americans complained long and loud and, when Beth left the ball eight feet short of the hole, Betsy called after Parkin, 'So, you think this is a playable green?'

In the meantime, Ali, who had been trying to play her little chip, called for quiet. The opposition did not like that and, though we won the hole to go four clear, they tore into us on the homeward stretch like a couple of wounded animals. The crowd were beginning to fear that our match was going to finish on a horribly anticlimactic note when Ali, bless her, holed a putt across the last green for the win. It had been a tough, tense match, one in which there was no love lost.

Lotta Neumann and Alfie, our all-Swedish combination, won the next game; their key stroke was the four wood they knocked over the ravine at the 16th at much the same time as we were finishing things off on the adjacent home green. Their victims were Dottie Mochrie, then the world's No. 1, and Pat Bradley.

But it was the all-Scottish pairing of Dale Reid and Pam Wright who were the real heroines of the hour. They had been three down with eight to play against Patty Sheehan and Juli Inkster but, thanks not least to their accompanying horde of Scottish supporters, the two Scots came roaring back into the match. A pitch by Pam to five feet at the 17th saw them level and, when Dale hit her second to 15 feet at the last, there was the chance that we might finish the day with a 3–1 lead. Sadly, Pam just missed across the sodden green, but we were still left with a 2½–1½, lead which was in itself a huge fillip.

At this stage, it was best that the excitement be contained. After all, we had been trounced in 1990 and everyone was well aware that the Americans could turn that first-day deficit into nothing more than a minor hiccup in the overall scheme of things.

On the following day, in the fourballs, Ali survived a telling off from Betsy King on the practice ground over what had happened at the 11th the day before. Betsy wanted to get it off her chest. The two of them are now good friends, but at the time it must have been alarming for Ali to be singled out in full view of a large section of gallery.

It was maybe as well that we were not playing against Betsy that day. Instead, after a two-hour delay for rain, we set out against Juli Inkster and Patty Sheehan. As everyone was saying, the rain suited me. The course was becoming so long that the par fives were probably out of range to everyone other than myself and Brandie Burton.

Ali's and my tactics were pretty basic. She would tee off first and hit one safely down the middle. I was then free to have an almighty smash at my tee shot.

We went ahead at the 5th, only for Juli to level the score with a birdie at the next. Not surprising at all. We had always expected that this would be a match as sticky as conditions underfoot.

As I remember it, the key hole was the 14th. The Americans had looked like going ahead, but I managed to hole a 20-footer and they missed a short one. That put us one up, and we then succeeded in making it two when I holed from double that distance at the 15th. It was one of those days – and thank God it coincided with a Solheim Cup – when I could not miss. Ali swears to this day that it was the best example she has ever seen of someone actually willing the ball into the hole, and I suppose that is how it was. I did it again at the last, holing from 14 feet for the match. We were round in 66.

Trish Johnson and Florence Descampe were more than grateful for their half in the second match. Brandie Burton had an eight-footer at the last for an American win, but the putt got away – and so did the putter, the implement disappearing over Brandie's left shoulder as she missed.

Pam and Dale lost a cracking match to Meg Mallon and Betsy King, who had been awesome over the front half, while the last match, between Lotta and Alfie and Pat Bradley and Dottie Mochrie, resulted in another half. A very important half. It had been a game which swung first one way, then the other. Europe were one up playing the last when Bradley, as she is wont to do in such circumstances, hit her approach close enough for a certain birdie. Alfie's approach was no more than five feet away, which meant that Lotta had this pressure-laden putt for a win. She missed and bent over double in her agony, her hands clasping her head.

Still, we were ahead 4½–3½, and the scene was set for what everyone was dubbing the most thrilling day of women's golf that Scotland had known since 1929 and the Joyce Wethered v. Glenna Collett final of the British Women's championship at St Andrews.

The Americans were clearly suffering mixed emotions at this point. They still thought they were going to come good in the singles but, at the same time, they were already looking for excuses. For example, they were complaining about the format over the first two days. They did not think it fair that two players from each side should sit out for both the foursomes and the fourballs. Catrin Nilsmark and Kitrina Douglas were the pair who sat on the bench on the first two days for us and, while they might not have liked it – who would? – they never said as much. They simply did what was expected of them and encouraged everyone else. It was a team effort, after all, and all of us – Europeans, that is – have had to sit out a match at some point or other in our golfing careers.

The Americans, on the other hand, had never known such an arrangement. Alice Miller did what she considered best in leaving no one out for more than the one day. Deb Richard and Brandie Burton missed the foursomes; Beth Daniel and Danielle Ammaccapane the fourballs. The first two went quietly enough, but Beth was always going to say what she thought about it. Her theory was that anyone good enough to make the team should be out there playing. They would win that argument. A new arrangement was brought in for The Greenbrier in 1994 whereby everyone played and each side brought a reserve.

There was no question of our team taking fright on the final day at Dalmahoy. Two years before, people said that we had sometimes looked positively apologetic when standing alongside the Americans on the practice ground. But on that Sunday morning at Dalmahoy we gave nothing but positive vibes to the eight thousand or so spectators who braved another grey and rain-spattered day.

Not long after the start, Mickey looked up at the board to see that there were more red (American) nameplates on the giant scoreboards than British blue. Let Mickey take up the story: 'I thought to myself, it's going to be tight. Then, the next time I glanced up, we were ahead in eight and down only in two. That's when I thought we would win, but I didn't fully take in that it was going to happen.'

I was out first and began precisely as I would have wished, clouting two woods to the heart of the green at the par-five 1st. One up after the 8th, I was brought back to square by a Burton eagle at the next which by all accounts had the American captain, Alice Miller, announcing to a party of Americans, 'That was the one we needed, right there!'

It could well have been a telling turning-point for the Americans, but I refused to allow it. I made a couple of awkward putts for halves before recapturing my lead with a birdie at the 12th. Then my putter rediscovered its mood of the previous day. I holed from 12 feet at the 14th and from 25 at the 15th. Charlie Mechem observed to someone at that point that if ever I were to get that fired up on tour, I would win millions upon millions of dollars.

Brandie hit into the undergrowth off the 16th tee and, after taking three to reach the green to my two, she ran on to the putting surface waving her white cap in lieu of a flag. The crowd loved that sporting gesture. Those who knew about it were still more touched when they learned how, after shaking hands, she had gone on running – up to her hotel room, where she could suffer in seclusion.

The second singles point came from Alfie, who survived a tension-packed start against Danielle Ammaccapane – seven halves in a row – before winning the next four holes on the trot. She tied things up on the 15th green, at which point she was three under par.

Next came Trish Johnson, who had started with a shaky six but, after that, was four under par in defeating the reigning US and British Open champion, Patty Sheehan, on the penultimate green. At that point, the scoreboard showed Europe with an overall tally of seven and a half points to America's three and a half.

Ali and Florence Descampe, playing fourth and fifth respectively, both came out on the losing side against their illustrious opponents but, back at the 15th, there were stirring cheers as Pam Wright put the finishing touches to a win over the legendary Pat Bradley. She had stormed past this great competitor with four birdies in five holes. The next win belonged to Lotta, who was three under par in defeating Betsy King.

Though Kitrina Douglas, who had not been played in the foursomes and fourballs, never really got into her stride against Deb Richard, the same did not apply to Catrin Nilsmark, who was similarly entering the fray for the first time. She outplayed the as yet unbeaten Meg Mallon and was three under the card and three up when they left the 15th green.

A few days later, at the Slovenian Open, Catrin was still talking of the once-in-a-lifetime scene which awaited her when she threaded her way through the crowd and on to the tee of the 16th, the hole where she would complete what was seen as one of the best wins of all time against the Americans in any of our fixtures with them.

'The entire fairway,' she recalled, 'was lined with people. I was not scared; I simply thought to myself, "This is our moment."'

To other eyes, not least my own, it conveyed the European tour's coming of age.

With Dale Reid having beaten Dottie Mochrie (now Pepper) in

the last match of the day, we had won by 11½–6½, a scoreline which I would recite to myself for weeks. What a party we had that night at Dalmahoy!

Did the Americans take the loss as badly as people made out? Yes and no, is the answer to that one. Alice Miller was one moment saying wonderful things about the Scottish spectators, the next moment ruining the effect of that generous tribute by suggesting that the spectators had been more sporting than the players. The assumption was that she was referring to what had happened in the match played by Betsy King and Beth Daniel against Ali and me. In all honesty, I think it was one of those occasions where both sides could have claimed to be in the right. The two of them had made a ridiculous fuss when they did not get the ruling they wanted, while we had maybe got too pumped up about the match as a whole.

When Juli Inkster was asked about what Miller had said, she replied, obliquely, 'Let's just say that your players behave very differently here than they do in the States.'

Several of the Americans had arranged Scottish holidays to tie in with the Solheim Cup week, and even if, as was alleged, Betsy was by then making out that the match wasn't all that important anyhow, you have to suspect that these vacations were not the merry affairs that had been intended.

All the squabbling did come across as a bit unseemly. But those at the helm were not surprisingly enjoying the mischief of it all. 'We have created a monster!' said Bob Cantin, from the Ping organization. There was more than a touch of glee in his voice, for he was thinking ahead to The Greenbrier in 1994.

2nd Solheim Cup

2–4 October 1992* The Dalmahoy Golf and Country Club* Edinburgh, Scotland

Foursomes
L Davies and A Nicholas beat B King and B Daniel 1 hole

L Neumann and H Alfredsson beat P Bradley and D Mochrie 2 & 1
F Descampe and T Johnson lost to D Ammaccapane and M Mallon 1 hole
D Reid and P Wright halved with P Sheehan and J Inkster
Foursomes: EUROPE 2½, USA 1½

Fourballs
L Davies and A Nicholas beat P Sheehan and J Inkster 1 hole
T Johnson and F Descampe halved with B Burton and D Richard
P Wright and D Reid lost to M Mallon and B King 1 hole
H Alfredsson and L Neumann halved with P Bradley and D Mochrie
Fourballs: EUROPE 2, USA 2

Singles
L Davies beat B Burton 4 & 2
H Alfredsson beat D Ammaccapane 4 & 3
T Johnson beat P Sheehan 2 & 1
A Nicholas lost to J Inkster 3 & 2
F Descampe lost to B Daniel 2 & 1
P Wright beat P Bradley 4 & 3
C Nilsmark beat M Mallon 3 & 2
K Douglas lost to D Richard 7 & 6
L Neumann beat B King 2 & 1
D Reid beat D Mochrie 3 & 2
Singles: EUROPE 7, USA 3

FINAL SCORE: EUROPE 11½, USA 6½

No doubt because of our victory at Dalmahoy, the American players and public alike were ready for us in White Sulphur Springs, West Virginia.

In the first place, they had chosen the ideal captain in JoAnne Carner. JoAnne, now in her mid fifties, is a player who, in amateur days, had a seemingly bottomless relish for the cut, thrust and fun of match-play. She had won the US Girls' championship, as well as the US Amateur, and she had been one of the greatest American Curtis Cup golfers of all time. She missed that side of the game when she started playing on the professional circuit, but now, at The Greenbrier, she had this wonderful chance to give vent to all her old instincts. One look at the hat she had got herself – a sequinned baseball cap featuring the stars and stripes – told how hyped up she was for the Solheim Cup.

In one of the pre-match press interviews, I was asked who I felt to be the best match player on the American side. My answer came out before I could stop myself; it was simply a matter of blurting out the truth.

'JoAnne Carner,' I said. The press chuckled at the way I had elevated the non-playing captain above the rest, and I could hardly blame them for making the most of it the next day.

But the best of the pre-match tales concerned the arrival of the American contingent. At five o'clock on the Monday evening, the buzz went round the photographers and television people waiting at the nearby Lewisburg Airport that the American team's plane had finally touched down. The cameras homed in on the plane – and out stepped a bunch of convicts, all of them handcuffed and bound for the state penitentiary!

Flag-raising ceremonies are always good for a story and this one was no exception. Pam Wright had no option but to haul aloft the flag of Novia Scotia (blue cross on white) because the flag firm had mistaken it for the Scottish flag which, of course, is white on blue. 'It's not mine,' Pam muttered, to those within earshot, before carrying on just the same.

Our uniforms, too, furnished quite a talking point. Anyone who was at The Greenbrier will remember the red, russet and golden glow of the trees. We simply don't get autumn colours of that intensity at home. It was this dramatic backcloth which maybe had most to do with the watery, wintry effect conveyed by our uniforms. They were pale pink and grey. 'The reverse of power dressing,' is how one critic put it, before going on to compliment the Americans on their bold red, white and blue.

I have often talked of my own, individual uniform problems,

from Surrey county up to Solheim Cup, and the last thing I would want to do here is to upset sponsors who were generous enough to have kitted us out. However, the players should have asked for more of an input and that is what we have had for the forthcoming match at St Pierre. In fact, I myself was at Marks and Spencer for a first meeting last November.

Helen Alfredsson had the honour of hitting the first ball in the opening foursomes series. She and Lotta were playing Dottie Mochrie and Brandie Burton. Helen completed her pre-shot shuffle and there followed a lovely clear boom through the remains of the morning mist. Her shot was a beauty.

Their match was a corker until the Americans made three birdies in four holes from the 12th on their way to winning to the tune of 3 and 2.

Annika Sorenstam and Catrin Nilsmark were two down after eight holes against Beth Daniel and Meg Mallon but, to their eternal credit, came back to win on the last green where Catrin holed a teasing three-footer. We then moved 2–1 ahead as Lora Fairclough holed the 15-footer bequeathed by Dale Reid's first-class tee shot to the short 17th.

Now it was Ali's and my turn. Against Donna Andrews and Betsy King we started with a birdie and went on to win by 2 and 1 to give Europe a 3–1 lead. Very satisfying. There were hopes that we might make it 4–1, but Trish Johnson and Pam Wright just came out on the losing side against Patty Sheehan and Sherri Steinhauer, the latter of whom played a great bunker shot at the last.

'If I'd been given 3–2 at the start of the day,' said Mickey Walker, 'I'd have grabbed it with both hands.' No one was surprised that she should make special mention of her two rookies, Annika and Lora.

If JoAnne Carner was upset by that first-day scoreline, she did not say as much. Foursomes, she maintained, were simply not the Americans' forte, but they would be back to normal for the next day's fourballs.

Ali and I were out top and we were up against Burton and

Mochrie on a day when Mochrie, as was reported at great length in the months which followed, went way over the top in competitiveness. She had offended me, slightly, the previous day in that when I went to congratulate her and Brandie on having beaten Lotta and Alfie, she had turned her back and hurried away.

She gave me a couple of less-than-friendly stares on the practice ground before our fourball, and there was trouble as early as the 1st hole. Dottie had hit from one bunker to another and from there over the green. She then chipped, exquisitely, and I said we were happy to concede the putt. I lobbed the ball across to her, gently, and she took a snatch of a catch before turning smartly on her heels and charging off the green. There was no hint of a 'Thank you'.

It was when I missed a 12-footer at the 3rd that she emitted an excited 'Yea!'. (She would say, later, that it was her way of reacting to the fact that they had levelled the match.)

After the game, which we lost on the penultimate hole, an American pressman asked, 'Did you talk to Laura about what happened at the 3rd?'

Her eyes like fireballs, Mochrie let fly at the poor fellow. 'Talk to *who* about *what*?' she demanded. 'Why should I?' As far as she was concerned, she had done nothing wrong.

Though we lost the fourballs 3–2, the manner in which we collected our second point had us finishing the day on a high rather than a low. After Dale and Lora had emerged triumphant in the third match, Lotta and Alfie arrived on the last green in a situation in which one of them had to make her birdie putt if they were to win. Lotta missed her eight-footer and now it was all down to Alfie. She is, as the whole world knows, a bit of a fidget, and every European supporter was a nervous wreck by the time she finally got down to the business of taking her putter away. She made it, however, and a relieved Mickey Walker described it as 'a huge psychological boost'. To recap, the score was now 5–5.

People poured out to watch a last day's play poised to go either way.

JoAnne Carner, great motivator that she is, had instructed her players to concentrate on winning the first. 'And if you can't win that,' she said, blithely, 'win the second.'

We were similarly confident, feeling that the matches had worked out well from our point of view, with the line-up as follows:

Betsy King v Helen Alfredsson
Catrin Nilsmark v Dottie Mochrie
Trish Johnson v Beth Daniel
Lora Fairclough v Kelly Robbins
Pam Wright v Meg Mallon
Alison Nicholas v Patty Sheehan
Laura Davies v Brandie Burton
Annika Sorenstam v Tammie Green
Dale Reid v Sherri Steinhauer
Lotta Neumann v Donna Andrews

Though Alfie, playing top, was to beat King, Mochrie wasted no time in making her mark on the afternoon. She was in no mood to be beaten by anyone at The Greenbrier, and she fairly ripped into poor Catrin Nilsmark in the second single. She made seven birdies in 13 holes and her supporters, who seemed to be at the same pitch of excitement as she was herself, let the whole of The Greenbrier know who was winning that one.

Dottie's start was mirrored by other members of her side. Beth Daniel won three of the first six holes against Trish; Kelly Robbins was four up after six against Lora; and Meg Mallon had three birdies in the first four holes against Pam Wright. Yet this was not as bad as it sounds. At midday, we were down in four, up in four and level in two.

Things were still as tight when Mickey Walker asked those manning the scoreboards if they would stop putting the all-square signs only on the American half of the boards, thereby making it look as if the Americans were up.

Almost before the scorers could act, the American players sorted it out themselves, going ahead in all those matches which had been square. Alfie apart, only Alison won for Europe on that last afternoon. My friend, Meg Mallon collected the crucial point for the home side.

I had been having a good return game with Brandie (we had played on the last afternoon at Dalmahoy) but, when I gathered that the overall match was lost, I felt hopelessly punctured. I knocked my approach into the lake at the 16th and lost by two holes. It was a match I would have won had I putted better, but, for some reason or other, I never got the hang of those Greenbrier greens. There was nothing wrong with them, but they did not suit me.

We had lost by 13–7, a bitterly disappointing scoreline. But it was not one into which anyone should have read too much. They out-putted us over the last nine holes in those singles, and that is all there was to it. Mind you, I know that others would have it that their class showed when it mattered.

To my way of thinking, things could just as easily have been the other way round. The two teams could not have been much more evenly matched.

The evening which followed was more than passing strange. We had lost, but we had enjoyed our week and were having a bit of a party. Catrin went to congratulate the Americans, only to find that they were all packing their clothes. They had done the business and now they were off to bed.

To us, this was rather sad. We rounded them up and insisted that they should celebrate and enjoy themselves.

3rd Solheim Cup

21–23 October 1994* The Greenbrier * White Sulphur Springs, West Virginia, USA

Foursomes
H Alfredsson and L Neumann lost to B Burton and D Mochrie 3 & 2
C Nilsmark and A Sorenstam beat B Daniel and M Mallon 1 hole
L Fairclough and D Reid beat T Green and K Robbins 2 & 1

L Davies and A Nicholas beat D Andrews and B King 2 & 1
T Johnson and Wright lost to P Sheehan and S Steinhauer 2 holes
Foursomes: EUROPE 3, USA 2

Fourballs
L Davies and A Nicholas lost to B Burton and D Mochrie 2 & 1
C Nilsmark and A Sorenstam lost to B Daniel and M Mallon 7 & 5
L Fairclough and D Reid beat T Green and K Robbins 5 & 3
T Johnson and P Wright lost to D Andrews and B King 3 & 2
H Alfredsson and L Neumann beat P Sheehan and S Steinhauer 1 hole
Fourballs: EUROPE 2, USA 3

Singles
H Alfredsson beat B King 2 & 1
C Nilsmark lost to D Mochrie 6 & 5
T Johnson lost to B Daniel 2 holes
L Fairclough lost to K Robbins 4 & 2
P Wright lost to M Mallon 2 holes
A Nicholas beat P Sheehan 3 & 2
L Davies lost to B Burton 2 holes
A Sorenstam lost to T Green 3 & 2
D Reid lost to S Steinhauer 2 holes
L Neumann lost to D Andrews 3 & 2
Singles: EUROPE 2, USA 8

FINAL SCORE: USA 13, EUROPE 7

Much has been written about the fact that the 1996 match at St Pierre is a twelve-a-side affair rather than ten. This suits the Americans, who feel they are stronger than us in depth, and though there was not an awful lot we could do about it, we maybe should not have given in without a fight. Mark you, I have to say that circumstances in the last two years have conspired to make the alteration much more acceptable. Since 1994, Europeans have made an incredible advance. Look at Annika, for example.

At the time of The Greenbrier, she had never won a tournament. Now she has several under her belt, including two US Opens. Annika, Lotta and I filled the top three berths on the Ping World Leaderboard for 1995, a year when we also had Ali Nicholas winning twice in America and Kathryn Marshall once. The Americans should be looking at our side and acknowledging that it is the strongest we have put out to date.

Now that the match is twelve-a-side, I do not think that it should be changed again. It is a facsimile of the Ryder Cup – and that, after all, is what we wanted.

* To date, I have played in three Solheim Cups and hated the uniform every time. At The Greenbrier, in 1994, I took one look and thought, 'What can I do to make this wearable?' The answer, I discovered, was to hide everything underneath my waterproofs. This year, at St Pierre, it is going to be different. Because I was among those who made a fuss at the last time of asking, I agreed to go on the committee to discuss what was needed for Wales. At St Pierre, the colours will be less wishy-washy and, hopefully, we will be wearing the clothes long after the match is done.

I don't think I have ever seen anyone out and about in the outfits we had for The Greenbrier. In fact, it was only recently I heard the tale of how a couple of our players had left their uniforms behind at the end of the week – and been appalled when the hotel sent them on.

Marks and Spencer were shocked at what we said about their last offerings, but they listened to our comments and said they would have no problem in providing what we want for the coming match. They made the point that things were bound to be better this time around in that we have given them so many more months in which to get organized.

It is not for me to say that it hurts my golf when I am not happy in what I am wearing. Aside from the fact that it sounds like an excuse, it is unfair on those who have furnished the outfits. Clearly, though, it does nothing to help the so-called feel-good factor. Whenever you take to the course, it makes sense to get as much right as possible before you get down to the business of playing the golf.

Chapter 14

No Place Like Home

The journalist who got Mum on the other end of the phone must have thought that I had my golf course in place already. 'She's hacking around in the rhododendrums,' is what Mum said. In fact, I had a pair of secateurs in my hand, rather than a wedge, and was trying to clear the undergrowth which covered most of the six acres when we moved into Northwood House during August 1994.

Now, almost two years later, the land has been tidied up and the rabbits have been sent packing, though a few of the little devils have so far outwitted us.

As you enter the iron gates from the leafy lane, there is a football pitch on your immediate right. By the time the new turf was laid, it had cost a little matter of £7,000. But it is by no means under-used. I am not remotely abashed to tell you that football ranks as my favourite hobby of the moment*. Any evening, when I

* **David Davies:** Laura's love of football had its origins in Tony's football beginnings when we were living in Marietta, Georgia. Tony, then eight to Laura's six, joined the junior league soccer and Laura, inevitably, wanted to be on the team, too. That was not on, so she somehow persuaded the organizers to give her a game on the YMCA's girls' side for 12-year-olds.

They made her a full-back, so she wouldn't get in the way, and I can am off the tour, the chances are that a game will be in full swing, usually involving golfers, caddies and my brother's friends. It may not be very ladylike and it may prompt some chat among the neighbours, but it is a fun way of keeping fit. I could never follow the same routine as some of the other golfers, who spend three or four hours a day in the gym, though some of my friends did get me to make a start earlier this year.

Beyond the football pitch, there is a practice net which, you may not be surprised to learn, has seen more cricket balls than golf balls.

Follow the driveway up to the house and there is a little roundabout in the shape of an old-fashioned well with, courtesy of my mum, flowers cascading around its edge.

Among a yardful of cars, a red Ferrari 456, is probably first to catch the eye. They say it's best to look at it while it is standing still because — although the stories all grow in the telling — I am accused of travelling too fast to be much more than a blur. The theory stems mainly from one of my sorties on a German autobahn where there is no speed limit. I made the mistake of admitting that I had once touched 162 mph. (It felt as if we were flying.)*

Closer to home, I once reduced the journey from Ottershaw to Dalmahoy to little over five hours. I had left Ottershaw at nine

---

see her now, standing there, hands on hips, glaring at all and sundry because the ball never came to her.

Then, at last, she had it. She dribbled it up through the entire field, scored a goal and said, 'So there,' or words to that effect. After that, they made her a forward.

* **David Davies:** I know where Laura's love of speed and fast cars comes from, too. Dolls never got a look-in in her young life. When Tony started collecting Dinky cars, she followed suit.

When Tony wanted a bicycle, they both wanted bicycles. We lived at the top of this hill and the two of them would hurl themselves down it and see who could come to the most sudden stop before the main road. As I would learn, from a neighbour, there was one occasion when Laura, then six, went hurtling straight across the main road and landed head over heels in the ditch on the far side.

o'clock and Mum had told someone in Edinburgh to expect me between four and five o'clock. In fact, I was there by 2.30.

It was on a return trip from Dalmahoy that I was once stopped by the police. My heart sank.

'Congratulations,' began the officer. Though he obviously meant me to wonder if this was some tongue-in-cheek reference to my setting a new record in terms of speed, he soon broke into the widest of smiles. He said he was referring to our win in the Solheim Cup. I suppose I had better emphasize that he went on to warn me that I was going a shade fast.

Another little confession I should make is of the time I horrified my dad by ringing from my mobile and saying, 'Dad, I'm up to 140 mph.' Very sensibly, he slammed the phone down on me. I then had no option but to ring again and say I was exaggerating. (I doubt if I was).

A Toyota 4 × 4, one of the fruits of my first win in the Itoen Ladies' Classic in Japan, is ready and waiting to transport the dogs, King Charles spaniels by name of Ben and Dudley, to the starting-point for their next walk. Then there is a large camper van which goes to tournaments played reasonably close to home. Sometimes, as at last year's English Open at The Oxfordshire, I will stay in it, but for the most part my parents will use it to entertain friends who come to watch. Since it is impossible to get clubhouse tickets for everyone you would like to get them for, especially for an event like the Weetabix British Open, the camper van provides the perfect alternative base.

A Triumph Herald, lovingly restored, albeit not by me – I can do little more than change a wheel and check the oil and water – peeps out of one of the garages. I must also give a mention to the tractor which has served so well over the last couple of years in our clearing of the garden.

In the States, I have a Ford van which, to my father's consternation, spends most of its time in his driveway. When he was over for Christmas last year, he was asking if it was sensible to be hanging on to a vehicle which, at best, gets three outings a year

Beyond the cars and the garages there is more garden, consisting of a pitch and putt course designed by Richard Crocker. A single, two-tier green, measuring 50 feet by 40, is the focal point, with, beneath it, a bunker built with bricks of turf in the manner of the traps at Muirfield where I played in the 1984 Curtis Cup. (I hope they don't have a patent on the design.) There are nine different tees placed round about which make for holes ranging in length from 40 to 100 yards. I should perhaps keep this one a secret, but there is a 10th tee, one which no one would want to use other than me. It is down by the football pitch and asks for a shot struck bang over the chimney tops. 'And what happens,' came the inevitable question from my father, 'if you break a window?'

'I replace it,' I replied. He shrugged his shoulders, because there was not much else he could do about this recalcitrant woman in her thirties. (Though he perhaps does not know this yet I have already hit a ball through the window of my mother's and Uncle Mike's new conservatory.)

Since our home is called Northwood House, we had a little bit of a problem with the name of the course. Northwood GC would have been ideal but, of course, there is one already – the establishment which emerged so badly from that *Cutting Edge* television programme of not so long ago. Hence I have had to go over the top a bit in calling my little folly the Northwood Golf and Country Club.

Mum thought I had taken leave of my senses when I ordered score cards of the course and tee boxes, but these little extras can only add to the fairy-tale fun of the place.

Going back past the garages to the house, which has a part brick, part tiled frontage, you take a left turn beyond the well towards the front door.

We have a door-keeper, an enormous brown teddy bear from Bentalls who sits on the left of the entrance and delights every young visitor, especially my godchildren. He is just one of a pack of around 100 bears that I have collected over the years. The latest recruit, incidentally, dwarfs this Bentalls bear and, for that matter, the rest of us as well. We spotted him in Harrods in December 1995. The store had this glorious gathering of Christmas bears, all of them identical in every respect save size. The six-inch ones were cute but, at the other end of the spectrum, the lone eight-footer was irresistible. Mum looked at the price tag and said it was less than she had imagined. I didn't need any more encouragement. We had to have him.*

The hall had a lovely expanse of wooden flooring when we moved in, but we have since had it carpeted. The reason we did this was because of Ben and Dudley. The wood seemed to act as a magnet for their hairs and there were days when it seemed that we had enough to cloak a third dog.

My mum and Uncle Mike have the lounge on the far side of the hall. They have added the aforementioned conservatory from which they can see the football at the end of the garden. And if they don't want to watch, I'm afraid they can hear it.

`To the left of their lounge is our communal kitchen, with a stable door which will eventually lead into the games-room I have in mind. At the moment, the games-room is still at the drawing-board stage. I could build it now, but I think it better to get a few more wins under my belt in order to make sure that I can afford to do it properly. What I want, I very much fear, is going to cost in the region of £200,000.

What I see, in the mind's eye, is an indoor swimming pool, a jacuzzi and a sensibly secure trophy room where I can put out the various cups, clubs and other mementoes I have acquired over the years. It will take in every putter and every driver I ever used. For all our differences, they are like old friends.

The kitchen has units of natural wood, and anyone who chooses to do a bit of tidying up around the sink will have an angled view

---

* **Rita Allen:** Laura is an impulse buyer and I'm afraid to say that I'm a bit that way myself. I don't usually comment if I think she is wasting money but, just occasionally, I am moved to try and put my foot down. It's probably because I don't do it too often that she takes a bit of notice.

Our one big difference was over the Ferrari. She wanted one; I thought it would be a criminal waste of money. To my mind, a Ferrari is something you get when you've got everything else you want, and Laura wanted her games-room. I lost that one, the Ferrari arriving at the door in mid-June.

over the tennis court, complete with practice wall. People roared with laughter when one with my reputation for doing as little golf practice as possible ordered a practice wall, but I love going out there to put in a bit of work on my backhand. Steffi Graf, whom I met at last year's Wimbledon, handed me a huge can of practice tennis balls when she heard that I had a tennis court. She didn't, though, accept my offer of a commensurate supply of golf balls. She said that she had tried golf and that it was too slow a game as far as she was concerned.

There is a hatch through the kitchen into a generous dining area and, beyond that, through an archway, is my own lounge, where the walls are covered with favourite pictures. Starting on the near wall, as you come in, there is a framed photograph of Desert Orchid. I went to watch his last race when he fell at Kempton Park. Below him, courtesy of an Irish trainer, is one of a mare named after me. As far as I know, she has never done anything much, but she certainly looks the part.

After the horses, there is a long, long window-sill housing one crystal golf trophy after another. Among them are my mementoes from the Solheim Cup, my Irish Open trophy and the glass replica I got for winning the Australian Open.

Moving on to the fireplace wall, there is my all-time favourite photograph: one of Ali and me playing together in the Solheim Cup we won at Dalmahoy. Alongside, there are photographs of my 1987 US Open win and my second major, the 1994 McDonalds, and another picture I love – of a group of us in Australia a couple of years ago. It includes the Lunns, Karen and Mardi, who have been friends almost from the first day they arrived on the European tour from Australia, and Lisa Hackney. Lisa is a former English amateur international who went to university in Florida before joining the tour. She is engaged to a teaching professional.

Other pictures of me include a couple of caricatures, which people have sent to us, and a front cover from *Golf World*, published in the week following the McDonald's.

However, the prime position in the room, bang above the middle of the fireplace, goes not to any golfing memento but to Desert Orchid. And it's not a picture but a beautifully crafted bronze model which I purchased from a catalogue for £600.

Leading off the lounge is the billiard-room, which similarly has a host of happy pictures and posters up on the walls, including one of my great hero, Freddie Couples. A large, stuffed hedgehog peeps rather apologetically out from under the table. I once nominated him as my most ridiculous extravagance of all time.

I won't bother taking you upstairs. Suffice to say that there are five bedrooms and four bathrooms, with all the bedrooms enjoying a lovely view over garden and trees.

One way and another, it is very difficult to pack my bags and leave when I have another run of tournaments ahead. Then I remind myself that if it weren't for golf, I wouldn't have a place like this at all.

Chapter 15

The Caddie Club

Every year, Laura invites all her caddies, past and present, to a Christmas luncheon. The latest of these took place at Sutton Green Golf Club on Thursday 21 December 1995. The guest-list on that occasion was as follows: Dave Davies (father); Mike Allen (stepfather); Rita Allen (mother); Tony Davies (brother); Matthew Adams (cousin and current caddie); Joe Marinas (family friend); John Barnard (landlord of Castle Inn in Ottershaw); Mark Fulcher (ex-caddie and friend).

Below, some of Laura's bag-carriers, along with Laura herself, record their favourite moments.

1985 Belgian Open Royal Waterloo

LD: This was my first win as a professional. I was three shots behind Maxine Burton with five holes to go, and someone came up to me and said, 'Don't worry, you'll have loads of other chances over the years.'

I thought to myself, 'Sod that!' and went on to finish eagle, birdie, birdie over Royal Waterloo's three closing par fives.

1986 British Women's Open Royal Birkdale

LD: I was dying to phone my mother to tell her that I had just won, but there was so much hullabaloo in the clubhouse that I had to stop at a call box 300 yards down the road. Mum did her best to sound stunned and delighted, but she eventually had to concede that someone had already rung with the good news. They had heard it on the radio.

Tim Clark: Laura was dreadful in practice. She often could be. In fact, I have the feeling that she walked in half-way through one of the practice rounds. She's just one of those people who cannot get interested until the gun goes.

My abiding memory is of our birdie, eagle start on the final day. At the 2nd a par five, she needed nothing more than a nine iron for her second shot. It flew with the wind and came down next to the flag to give her a tap-in three. Having gone from behind to in front over those two holes, we then moved further ahead.

As we stepped on to the tee at the 12th we were three clear. It was at that moment, to my horror, that one of Laura's friends came up and said, 'What does it feel like to be the Open champion?' I don't need to spell out how I felt about that little interruption. I did my best to get rid of the girl as quickly as possible.

I feared the worst when Laura belted her ball into a greenside trap and then took three putts, to have her lead cut to one. At the next, my heart started to pound even more, not least because she had gone into what I call her 'fast forward' mode. She took an iron off the tee for safety, only to catch another bunker. Thankfully, this was a par five and, though she played the hole almost on the run, she did not drop a shot.

By the 16th, things had calmed down. More importantly, the advancing Marta Figueras-Dotti had fallen away. Our lead was back at two shots, and we more or less completed our week's work with a birdie at the 17th.

It was fun-going down the last. The scenes matched those at a men's Open as the crowds swept down the fairway rather than behind the ropes. I remember a little boy – he was probably about eight or nine – coming up to ask if Laura's bag was heavy. I slipped it over his shoulder for a few yards so that he could find out.

Looking back, arguably the most extraordinary thing about Laura's win was that it was over a links course. Yes, the weather was good, but there was still a good measure of wind, and Laura, at that point, was not a particularly solid wind player. I had known courses where, when it started to blow, she would simply go further and further off line.

At that point in Laura's career, caddies and players were more like friends than employees and employers. Where Laura stayed that week was no better than where the caddies were staying – just a humble boarding house.

The Open was the start of a five-week spell in which we would win three times. The most important victory was the one at La Manga, because it was there, in what was the final tournament of the season, that Laura overtook Lotta Neumann to win the Order of Merit.

1987 US Open Plainfield

Tony Davies: Caddying in the States was something I hadn't done before and it was all a bit daunting. I was probably more nervous than Laura, but I picked things up as I went along. She won on an 18-hole play-off, but the last hole of the fourth round is the one which I can still picture as clearly as the day she played it. Laura was tied for the lead and, after her tee shot, she walked a good 150 yards to look at the leaderboard by the green to see how JoAnne Carner, up ahead, had finished.

JoAnne, as it turned out, had had a bogey, and Laura knew, then, that a closing birdie would be good enough. The same applied for Ayako Okamoto, with whom we were playing.

Everything was horribly quiet as Laura played her second. We had opted for a hard-hit eight iron and, bearing in mind that she had never played at at this lofty level before, she came up with a beauty. The ball finished around 20 feet from the flag.

Then we had to go through mental torture as she putted up to four feet and had to hole that four-footer to get into the play-off.

Another thing that sticks in my mind is the little exchange which took place between Laura and JoAnne Carner at the 17th hole in the play-off. The 17th was playing at 493 yards and had a hill rising steeply from the tee which meant that, even for Laura, there was no view of the green when she was playing her second. Although there were club members who had sworn that it could not be done by a woman, Laura had caught the green twice in the first three days, and now she was determined to do it again.

This time, she asked for her three wood and, against a background of excited whispers, she smashed the thing over the hilltop and on to the putting surface – a particularly risky shot here in that she could so easily have lost most of that distance by catching the brow of the hill.

As the cheers told that the ball was safe, Laura and I heard JoAnne laughing a throaty laugh. 'Why on earth would you have tried that?' she asked.

'No brains!' returned Laura.

That was my first win with Laura, the biggest and the best.

1987 British Open St Mellion

Tim Clark: Although Laura didn't win – she finished second – it still added up to a week to remember. The week before, she had won the US Open. Thrilled though I was for Laura, I myself had been going through hell because Tony was carrying the bag rather then me.

As she was flying back with the trophy, I was pacing out St Mellion, because she was not going to have time for a practice round. When she began on the first day, I could not believe the way she was hitting the ball. It was as if she had reached a new level during her week in America.

We were one behind after 16 holes of the last round, and the excitement mounted still further as Laura laid into what was the perfect drive down the 17th. She asked me if I agreed with her choice of a wedge for her second shot and, very stupidly, I nodded, for I knew, deep down, she needed a nine iron. She took the wedge and, though it reached the green, it left her so short that she three-putted.

Because I had received so much stick about Laura's US Open win, with everyone jesting that she had done better with me out of the way, I was desperate to win at St Mellion.

There was still the chance that we might birdie the last and force a play-off, but Ali Nicholas got down in a chip and a putt to win. I had thought she might miss her four-footer, but Ali is a great little competitor and she never looked like missing.

1988 Tucson Open Randolph Park

LD: To me, this was as important as any title I ever won. After my US Open win in 1987, the LPGA had amended its constitution in order that I could have automatic membership. By winning in Tucson, I think I proved that I deserved that honour. My US Open win could no longer be dismissed as a fluke.

1989 Lady Keystone Open

Matthew Adams: There was a picture of Laura and me in the newspaper on the day after this win. I was holding the flag-pole and, at the same time, jumping sky high. It summed up to perfection how excited I was at the end of a tournament in which Laura had finished birdie, birdie, birdie to beat Pat Bradley.

The 16th was a par five, where she was on in two and left herself with a little tap-in for the first of that trio of birdies; the 17th was a par three, where she holed a 25-footer; the 18th deserves a bit of extra detail . . .

Pat Bradley had hit her tee shot into the trees on the right and had to chop out with her second.

Laura caught the putting surface in two but was not particularly pleased with the shot. She had taken a nine iron for the 165 yards because she was feeling so pumped up, and, almost unbelievably, even that proved a little much, the ball coming to rest on the back left-hand edge of the green. She then stood by and watched Bradley's third which, typical Bradley, was wellnigh perfect.

I can remember Laura saying, 'She's bloody holed it!' The

crowd were thinking the same but, mercifully, the ball pulled up three feet away.

Laura's putt turned out to be a 50-footer, and now she simply had to get down in two to force a play-off. To my surprise, for this was only the second time I had caddied for her, she had up until then been asking me to help with the reading of the greens. On this occasion, though, she did not want any assistance. 'It's OK,' she said, 'I've got this one.'

She had. It rolled bang into the middle of the cup, and the moment it dropped was when I leapt skywards. We had won by a shot.

1991 Valextra Classic Olgiata

LD: I very nearly abandoned ship after a few holes of the final day. I had this terrible upset stomach and had to keep diving into the bushes. Luckily, there was a doctor – a gynaecologist – in the crowd. He came to my rescue with some pills which worked within the space of a couple of holes. I don't know what people must have been thinking, but at that point I didn't care.

From the ninth hole onwards, I felt able to concentrate on the golf.

1991 Inamori Classic Stoneridge County Club

LD: This was a win with a difference, in that I never once used my driver off the tee but stayed with a two iron. I had been hitting the driver badly for some time and only had to touch it to have this nightmare feeling that I was going to blast the ball straight right. The American papers had a field day writing up that win. They couldn't believe that anyone could win an LPGA tournament using nothing but an iron off the tee.

1992 AGF Open de Paris Golf de la Boulie

Rita Allen: This was a tournament run in conjunction with a men's event. Laura finished joint second with Cathy Panton behind Sue Strudwick, but my main recollection is of running over Gilliam Stewart's clubs with the electric trolley. To set against that, there was a lovely moment when I was waiting under a tree and this ball dropped down beside me. It belonged to Fred Couples and, when I showed him where it was, he said 'Thanks ma'am' and touched his cap.

1992 European Open Golf Club Beverberg

LD: The first of my wins after reinstating my driver. I had got back together with the club in Las Vegas after reaching the turn in 46 in the first round. On the grounds that things could get no worse, Tony very wisely suggested that this was as good a time as any to give the driver a run. I cold-topped it off the 10th tee and banned it from the course for another six months, but that was the start.

I kept on hitting it well on the range but, the moment I took it out for real, I would have this horrific blocked shot in my mind. I asked Dave Regan's opinion about this, and it tallied with my own – that I should start making myself use the club again in competition and play through this mental block, for that is what it was.

Things began to get a little better, and the ultimate test came when I was seven shots ahead in the European Open and started blasting the ball right again. My lead began to dwindle and so did my confidence. I simply had to get a good drive away at the last if I was going to win the thing – and I did. That shot, more than any other, marked my return.

1992 Holiday Inn Leiden Open Rijs

Rita Allen: Laura finished second, but the excitement of the competition was rather lost on me. I remember feeling utterly confused at one point. Laura was bolting around the place and I hadn't a clue where to go. On the very first hole in the final round, I walked off the green with the flag in my hand and Laura turned to me and said, 'Are you going to collect all eighteen?'

1993 McDonald's LPGA Championship Dupont Country Club

Mark Fulcher: From my point of view, Laura's finest win. Its seeds were sown the week before as we were flying to the States from Japan. I was fast asleep when suddenly I found myself being shaken awake. It was Laura. She had something to tell me. She said that, as from that day, she was not going to moan on the golf course. If, say, she hit into trees, she wasn't going to say she had been unlucky. She was going to accept that the ball was in the trees because that's where she had hit it.

When she teed up in the McDonald's, she stuck to what she had said, even though she was sorely tried as early as the start of the second half of her first round. She had turned in four under par, but at the 10th her ball had caught a fairway bunker which had not been raked. Her lie was shocking. I waited to see how she would react, but she simply shrugged her shoulders and said, 'My fault for hitting it here.'

She got it out to within 50 yards of the green, hit her next to ten feet and slotted the putt for a four. Before, in those circumstances, we would have been looking at a five, maybe more. Her round that day was a 66.

In the last round, she was one shot ahead with three to play when everything stopped because of thunder and lightning. We had an hour's break and she knew, when she got back, that she needed three pars to win.

She got them at the 16th and 17th, but then missed the green with her second to the last.

'Looks like it'll be a play-off,' she said.

I knew she didn't mean it. She chipped to ten feet and holed.

It was the most exciting five seconds of my life. If I were ever to caddie for the winner of the British Open, it couldn't be better than that.

During the tournament, she had said that if we were to win, she would give me the watch of my choice as well as a 10 per cent bonus. (Laura always gives 10 per cent of her purses, regardless of whether she has won. Other professionals tend to give 7.5 per cent of their winnings for anything other than first place, but one day Laura said she couldn't be bothered working out 7.5 per cent, so she would simply make it ten.)

The watch I chose was a TAG Heuer worth around $1,000, and since then she has given the same one to others.

1993 Australian Masters Royal Pines

Mark Fulcher: As I remember it, we were leading by one going into the last round. We had an hour and a half in hand when we got to the course, which was really too much because the players had to take a cart to get to the practice round and Laura cannot be bothered with that kind of hassle. In fact, she never went to the range all week.

We had killed the time easily enough on the previous days, but that day it was passing slowly. 'Let's have a set of tennis,' she suggested.

We had a set and she beat me. Then we took a courtesy car back to the hotel in order to change and have a shower before her tee-off time.

Her warm-ups that day consisted of three turns of her elbows behind her back and a handful of putts. Then she went out and had a 68, to win by a shot.

No, I did not protest at any of those extraordinary preliminaries. If it had been someone other than Laura, I might have been moved to say something, but Laura is unique.

1994 Sara Lee Classic Hermitage Golf Club

Mark Fulcher: It was here, at the Hermitage's par-five 11th, that I saw Laura play the finest shot I have ever seen her hit. The hole had water down the left and in front of the green, and Laura, on this occasion, took her driver and smashed the ball right. It finished in a greenside bunker on the adjacent 17th hole. She looked at me and said, 'How far to the green?'

'Two hundred yards,' I replied, a little stunned.

'Do you fancy it?' she asked.

I was too stunned to say anything, but followed instructions in handing across her two iron. She hit it on to the heart of the green, and the crowd, like me, couldn't believe what they were seeing.

1995 Chik-Fil-A Charity Championship Eagle's Landing

Joe Marinas: I used to play with Laura when she was an amateur, and we carried on having the occasional game long after she turned professional. Her length made me sick but I always enjoyed watching her.

Since I do the estimating in a painting and decorating business owned by one of Laura's uncles, I was very caught up in her progress. It was at the 1984 British championship, when she was still an amateur, that I stepped in to caddie for her for the first time. Tony, her brother, had done the first two rounds, but he had this terrible problem with a tooth and could not finish the tournament.

I was nervous then, but nowadays, on the rare occasions when I caddie for her, I'm only a little nervous at the start. I hadn't seen Laura play for a couple of months when I got to Atlanta, and the first thing to strike me was how well she was hitting everything, right through the bag. The course was made for her. For instance, there was this tricky par four, a hole of 298 yards, which everyone else was playing as a dog-leg.

Laura, of course, asked for her three wood on each of the three days and hit over the tree-tops. We caught the green twice and emerged with two birdies and a par.

However, the hole where she won the tournament was the 10th. There had been this long delay for rain, and the first shot we had to play on our return was one over water. Everything was sodden. We had been going to take a six but we decided on a five and it only just made it over the water. Had we dropped a shot there, we might have been in trouble.

As it was, we made our par and, by the time we got to the 15th no one could touch us.

She gave me my usual fee, plus a percentage and a present. Like the rest of her winning caddies, I got my TAG Heuer watch. I also had a lot of fun.

What did we talk about on the way round? Gambling, of course.

1995 Irish Holidays Open St Margaret's Golf and Country Club

Matthew Adams: Laura was in cruise control for this event. She won by 16 shots and she could have won by more. There are times when she has this ability to blow a field, and this was one of them.

It was scary. The putts would drop almost without her reading them. I knew, when she was six ahead on Friday, that this was it. By Saturday, she was nine ahead and 19 under. This was the point at which she tried to come to an arrangement with the book-makers re her eve-of-the-tournament bet that the winning total would be 19 under. The bookie, no doubt suspecting that Laura's professional pride would take over, did not want to know. He was right enough. Laura galloped further under the card and went on to win the tournament by a massive 16 shots.

Ireland had something to do with it. Laura loves the people and she loves playing there. I have seldom seen her so relaxed.

Chapter 16

Question Time

In this final chapter I am going to deal with the questions I am asked the most frequently about golf and my golfing life.

1. *How do you hit it so far?*

That is definitely the No. 1 question, one which probably crops up five times more often than any other. I used to say that I didn't have a clue but, over the years, I think I have got to the bottom of it. It is a combination of broad shoulders, strong legs, brute force and timing. I must stress that strength alone isn't everything. If it were, Colin Montgomerie would hit it farther than he does.

2. *Were you a long hitter from the start?*

When I started, I either belted the ball or missed it altogether. I wanted to hit hard so that I could keep up with my brother and his friends. That was all that mattered.

3. *Do you feel pressure when playing alongside women professionals such as Michelle McGann who are sometimes billed as being as long as you are?*

No, not nowadays. In fact, I have a new Maruman driver which has cost me a few yards but with which I seldom miss a fairway. I have been outdriven a few times since I started using this club, but I long ago accepted that sheer length does not win tournaments.

Mind you, if it suddenly mattered to me that I should get one past everyone, it would be easily done. If the fairway were nice and open, I would aim well right and put a touch of draw on the ball. That's where my really big one – the 280–300 yarder – generally comes from.

4. *Were you as long as Ian Botham when you played together?*

No, I am afraid not. He is very much a one-off in that he hits everything around the 300-yard mark. The shot can be down the middle, but it is just as likely to be 300 yards straight right or 300 yards straight left. All his shots seem to head directly for where they end up. It's very strange but, at least when I was playing with him, there was never any hint of slice or draw. I have never seen anyone tear into the ball as he does.

5. *Were you longer than Nigel Mansell?*

Just a bit – not a lot.

6. *Would you advise youngsters to hit hard from the start?*

Yes, they are much better off learning to give the ball a good crack. You want young people to experience the joy of fearless hitting, although they have to learn to recognize their maximum strike. If they go beyond that they will lose balance and length.

7. *What's the best advice you can give to parents?*

This is a difficult one. My own parents never put pressure on me, but they are always around to give encouragement and support. I don't know whether I would have done as well without it.

The Welsh Golf Union put out an excellent sheet not long ago entitled 'Parents are important, too'. Under the heading 'Some Dont's', the one which caught my eye began: 'Don't allow the situation to develop where your child is frightened of playing poorly because of the way you respond . . . A fear of failure can often result in children feigning injury, avoiding certain competitions or playing with unnecessary caution.'

I much approved, too, of the item suggesting that parents should not force a young child to specialize entirely in golf. 'Children,' it said, 'should be allowed to develop their own preferences. In any case, up to the age of 15 or 16, a concentrated diet of only one of golf, tennis, or whatever, is hardly going to enhance a child's enthusiasm for the sport in question.' Another point worth digesting was along the lines that it was wrong for parents to turn a blind eye to any bad behaviour, cheating, or bad manners by their child. It suggested that prompt action was appropriate: 'To do otherwise would infer that you condone such behaviour or at least that you do not consider personal standards and respect for people and rules important in sport.

The last item was one exhorting parents not to say, 'we' won or 'we' lost. The advice, here, was that parents should remember that it is the child who is participating and that they are there to support and to encourage. 'The progress of many junior golfers,' it stated, 'has been hindered by excessive parental involvement.'

The item finished as follows: 'Parental example is so important . . . After all, if *you* cannot cope with the ups and downs of your children's golfing life, how can you expect *them* to cope?'

8. *What do you thing of all the old-fashioned rules at golf clubs?*
Well, I don't agree with the men-only clubs, for a start. I can't believe they will exist much longer. One of my favourite courses is Muirfield, where I played in the 1984 Curtis Cup. However, were I to hammer on the door and ask if I could have a round with a couple of my friends, they would have a fit. It's all very well to say that women are allowed to play if they are with one of the members, but that strikes me as a little patronising.

On the subject of rules about juniors, I feel very sore about those which stop kids from playing in the adults' competitions. As I have mentioned elsewhere in these pages, I was once told I didn't qualify for a medal spoon because my parents were only paying a junior subscription for me.

Having said that, I am not against the club being strict with the juniors over how they behave and what they wear around the place. In fact, I have always thought that parents who take their offspring's side in any row along those lines are not really doing the child any favours.

9. *Who has been the biggest influence on your golf?*
My brother, Tony. He had a good swing for me to copy, and that, I think, has contributed most to the way I play today. Had Tony had a bad swing, I might have started off on entirely the wrong lines.

10. *Do your parents play?*

My father, Dave, has been down to a single-figure handicap and still plays a useful game out in the States. Mum never played at all until a few years ago. We've taken her down to the driving range a few times, but she has never exactly got hooked. Now that we have a little course in the back garden, it could be a different story.

11. *Is there a terrible sameness about golf on tour?*

Not at all. In the first place, the golf itself, with the different courses and conditions, will ask new questions every day. Then, even before you tee up at the first, there is the business of how you are feeling. Some days, you will have the sensation that there is nothing you want to do more than to hit your opening drive; others, you will be feeling only half like it.

You will then be influenced by how you play. On the very day you felt you could not wait to start, you might open with a bogey and be totally punctured. Equally, the day which had unpromising beginnings can turn into one of the best. It's not a life in which you can afford to sit back and let things happen. You have got to make them happen.

12. *Do a lot of the women professionals fall for their caddies?*

I think I can safely say that there is quite a bit of carrying on between the two parties.

13. *Are there a lot of lesbians in women's golf?*

People always get round to this question eventually – and ever more so since the extraordinary case of Ben Wright, the British CBS commentator who was removed from the women's side of things earlier this year following his comments in the *News Journal of Wilmington* on the morning of 12 May 1995. What he said, among other things, was that lesbians on the American tour made it difficult for the LPGA to attract sponsorship and television coverage.

'Let's face facts,' said the article, quoting Wright. 'Lesbians in the sport hurt women's golf. It's paraded. There's a defiance in them in the past decade.'

Initially, Wright said he was 'disgusted at the pack of lies and distortion that was attributed to me in the newspapers this morning'. Some months later, though, Dan Jenkins, whom Wright had always seen as a good friend, wrote in *Sports Illustrated* that Wright had admitted to him that he had said these things.

My opinion on the lesbian issue, for what it is worth, is that their number in the world of women's golf has probably declined over the last few years. On the other hand, it would seem to me that there are far more in everyday life.

I would not want to pass judgement, but it strikes me that the newer generations of women professional golfers are very different from the old school. More often than not, a young girl arriving on tour will have a husband, a fiancé or a boyfriend in tow.

Charlie Mechem, then the American tour's Chief Executive, answered Wright's theory more than adequately when he said that no potential sponsor had ever cited lesbianism as a reason for withholding support: 'I do not believe that it is a significant issue for the LPGA or that it has impeded its growth in the past or that it will impede its growth in the future.'

Dottie Pepper, the hot-headed heroine of America's last Solheim Cup side, also had a very sane comment to bring to bear. 'We have breast cancer, divorce and everything else in society out here. We are just normal people.'

Nancy Lopez, on being asked for her views, came up with a counter-question: 'Why doesn't Wright talk about the men on tour who fool around on their wives?'

Lauri Merten, winner of the US Open at Crooked Stick, called the wretched Wright 'a jerk' and said that he should be fired. Which, of course, he was. The statement from David Kenin, the President of CBS Sports, was as follows: 'Ben Wright will not be part of CBS Sports' golf broadcast team when the Network's golf coverage begins with the AT&T Pebble Beach National Pro-Am (Feb. 3–4.)

'Because of the continuing controversy that has arisen from comments attributed to Wright, CBS believes his association with the Network has detracted from its golf coverage, as well as the focus on the players and tournaments.

'There are no plans for Wright's return to CBS Sports' golf broadcasts.'

How did I feel about his departure?

I suppose I felt a little sorry for the guy in that he had always appeared to be a good friend of the LPGA. I found it difficult to believe that someone of his stature would say such things, but I know myself that, when you have an interested audience, it is easy to get carried away. We all say things we regret from time to time. Myself, I once launched an entirely unnecessary attack on Old Thorns, the Hampshire course where we played our Toshiba Players' championship in 1988. When I was asked what I thought about the greens, I described them as 'a nice shade of brown'. Then, warming to my theme, I think I suggested that a couple of them would benefit from being dug up.

Michael McDonnell, from the *Daily Mail*, was good enough to tell me to stop. My only regret is that he didn't tell me a little sooner. I must have hurt a lot of people's feelings that day, when I could so easily have found some good things to say about a course which was obviously the owners' pride and joy.

Elsewhere in the *News Journal of Wilmington* article, Wright referred to me as 'a casino rat', and 'a woman built like a tank'. In reply, I can only reiterate what I said on the morning all this broke: 'As to my physical appearance, I am not a fashion model and have never pretended to be one. I am a professional golfer. I am a big person. But to be called a tank in print is very harsh. It wasn't a very nice way to wake up at 6.15 this morning.'

At that time, when Wright was still maintaining that he had never said anything of the sort on any of these matters, people asked if he had ever come up to me to explain himself. The answer is that he never did. In his defence, I made the light-hearted suggestion that I had perhaps been tucked behind a flag-stick and he hadn't been able to see me.

Wright's final outburst was on the subject of women's busts. He maintained that women golfers were handicapped by this part of their anatomy. 'It's not easy,' he said, 'for them to keep their left arm straight, and that's one of the tenets of the game.'

It was left to me and Nancy Lopez to deal with this one. I said that there were some pretty good women golfers around and, as far as I knew, they all had breasts. As for Nancy, her reply to his allegation that 'boobs get in the way' was an unanswerable 'How does Ben know? He doesn't have any.'

14. *Do you have any tips on how to handle pressure?*

Sometimes, when I have a big shot to play, I will try for a facsimile of someone else's rhythm and timing. On top of that, I will sometimes hum a tune – rather as I did at a crucial point in my US Open. Golfers have been doing both these things for years. Take this passage from Pam Barton's book, *A Stroke a Hole*:

'It is as well to remember,' she wrote, 'that in pressure situations, the muscles of the body tend to lose their slackness. This will not do. A keyed-up mind is a good thing, but no good can come of tense legs, arms and shoulders. I guard against unnatural rigidity by fixing firmly in my mind the image of some perfect swing like, say, that of Archie Compston or Henry Cotton . . . Secondly, I will try humming. The tune will not be the first that comes into my head. Probably, it will be a waltz, lilting and rhythmic . . . The idea sounds absurd until you try it out.'

15. *Don't you get tired of playing in the rain in Britain?*

For some reason, this is the question which annoys me more than any other. I'm usually in the States when I have to field it, and I always feel like saying that the American weather isn't that great. I can honestly say that I've known far more tournaments interrupted by rain over there than here. When it's raining in Britain, you carry on as if nothing has happened. Over there, the siren sounds and you are brought in off the course because of the lightning. It can be very disruptive, especially when it happens two or three times a round.

Another point worth making is that Europeans seem to be better at handling extremes than their American counterparts. The Americans tend to slow down to a virtual standstill when it gets wet and windy, which does suggest that they are less able to take difficult conditions in their stride. Nor can they cope when it gets too hot. In fact, I would guarantee that on any day when the temperature shoots over the 90 mark, any American playing companion would start uttering complaints long before I would.

16. *Are professional golfers spoilt?*

Very definitely. The courtesy cars, the food in the locker-room and so on. We are pampered to a ridiculous degree.

You see it most at an event like the men's Johnny Walker in Jamaica. Last year, I watched good old Bernhard Langer grinding it out at a time when it seemed to me that the rest of them didn't give a damn. I admired Bernhard for that. You have to wonder why the others bother playing in these things if they are not going to try.

If I were a sponsor, I wouldn't put money into that kind of a farce. I would only invest in those events which counted towards the money list.

17. *What's the future of the women's tour in Europe?*

When people asked me that in the early 1990s, I used to sound a bit doubtful. At one point, our circuit was a skeletal 12-tournament affair which was hardly going to act as a magnet for new recruits either among players or sponsors. Then Terry Coates took over as our Chief Executive, and his belief in the women professionals transmitted itself to others. He paved the way for a 1996 American Express European Tour which was worth around £3 million. The Ping World Leaderboard tells its own story of the progress made by Europe's women professionals. At the time of writing, there were three Europeans at the top – myself, Annika Sorenstam and Lotta Neumann. To see that in black and white serves as a huge fillip in the months leading up to a Solheim Cup match.

18. *What's the most moving tribute anyone has ever paid you?*

It was in the shape of a letter from Charlie Mechem. He wrote it about two years ago, when he was into his third year as the Chief Executive of America's LPGA tour. He was thanking me for my contribution to their circuit, and his main point was to the effect that I always had time for everyone. It was signed by Charlie and his wife, Marilyn, and it meant so much to me that I put it in a frame and hung it on my bedroom wall.

19. *Would you advise my daughter to turn professional?*

I never know what to say to this one because, nine times out of ten, I will never have met the daughter, let alone seen her play golf.

20. *What's the best thing about professional golf?*

The competition.

21. *The worst?*

The travel.

22. *Who's the rudest golfer you ever met?*

Dottie Mochrie, now Pepper. Mind you, nowadays she is not as bad as she was. She seems to have mellowed in the past 12 months.

23. *What is your favourite memento?*

The replica I have of the Solheim Cup. These were presented to everyone who played in the inaugural match in 1990 at Lake Nona, and they say that they are never going to be made again. All my other glass trophies could tumble from the window sill and I would get over it. If this one were to fall, I would be shattered too.

Just how much it means to me can be gauged from the fact that, when I moved house in the summer of 1994, it was one of two things I didn't leave to the removal people but chauffeured on the front seat of my car. The other item was the model of Desert Orchid which stands on my mantelpiece.

24. *What is the most difficult thing you get asked to do as a champion?*

I am afraid I dread being asked to visit hospitals. At the Standard Register tournament, for example, they wanted me to visit the young cancer patients who benefit from the event's proceeds. I said I was sorry, but I would have to say 'No'.

I am not a natural when it comes to dealing with the sick. I simply hate to see people suffer. But there is something else which worries me as much, if not more. I have always loathed the kind of cheap publicity which is apt to attach to someone holding a sickly child.

Obviously it would do children good to see a celebrity like a Michael Jackson. That would give them a lift. But if I were to go along, they would be thinking, 'Who's she, swanning around here as if she's a somebody?'

If I received a personal request to go along and see a sick person, that would be entirely different. In those circumstances, I would go if I could, though I am not saying I would find it an easy thing to do.

25. *Are you superstitious?*

This sounds crackers, but at the start of a tournament, Matthew will look me out a cluster of white, wooden tees, a pencil and a marker, the latter being a coin from the country in which we are playing. At the end of a day, I will take them back to the hotel and leave them on my bedside table.

Come what may, I want to stick with this original selection and, if ever I were to forget this little pile in the morning, I would happily drive back eight, even ten miles to pick it up.

26. *What have been your biggest prizes and biggest extravagances?*

To date it would be the JCPenney/LPGA skins golf game, where I holed a record 12 foot putt to win a record £200,000. Apparently, that was the most money pocketed by anyone – man or woman – on one hole in such a contest. For the record, I finished the weekend with a total of £228,000.

Before that it would have been $165,000 for winning the 1994 McDonalds, although the easiest money was the $140,000 I got for finishing second in a skins game to Dottie Mochrie. As for my biggest extravagances – 18 television sets; a football pitch in front of the house costing around £7,000; a large stuffed hedgehog costing £150.

27. *Which courses do you like least and most?*

I'm not an admirer of some among the modern championship courses. They design them for the championships they hope to hold and the poor amateurs have to suffer for it.

I am a Jack Nicklaus fan but I cannot pretend that I like St Mellion. To my mind, it is awful – and not just for the players but the spectators. You only have to see what the men score round there every year to realize that it is over the top.

If I had to pick out my two favourite courses I think I would opt for Muirfield in Britain and Mission Hills in the States. It's a toss-up as to which I would put first.

28. *Is it true that you once had a lesson from one of David Leadbetter's men at Lake Nona?*

Not true, though I know exactly how the rumour arose. It was in 1990 at the US Women's Open at Atlanta. Someone from IMG came up and said that Mitchell Spearman, one of the Leadbetter professionals, would be walking nine holes with me that day. I said, 'That's nice,' and never thought anything more about it until the end of the round. That was when IMG said that they thought that Mitchell was the man to help me.

I thanked them very much but explained that I was not interested in taking lessons. I had always done things my way and, as Vivien Saunders would confirm from the days I was sent to her for England's squad training, I'm no good at being told what to do. As everyone knows, my way is to copy people – and the people I copy are those who I know can do things better than I can do them. People like Seve Ballesteros, Freddie Couples, Bernhard Langer etc.

Another plus about being your own coach is that you don't have anyone to blame but yourself when things go wrong. That is obviously no bad thing.

29. *Have you ever smoked?*

No. My parents take the credit for this. They will tell you that they put me off smoking through being smokers themselves.

30. *Do you wear glasses?*

Yes, for watching television. To be honest, I can't see the end of most of my shots on the course.

31. *What did the Queen say when she gave you your MBE?*

She knew I was going to France the next day for a tournament and she told me to keep up the good work. I don't know whether anyone ever pointed it out to her, but I followed instructions and went out there and won.

Appendix

Laura Davies's Career
Record

Amateur career

1981
Scratch handicap.

1982
Plus one handicap. Surrey Junior Champion.

1983
Plus two handicap; English Intermediate champion; semi-finalist in English championship; fourth in British Women's Stroke-Play championship; Welsh Open Stroke-Play champion. South Eastern champion. Member of winning England team in European Junior Team championships.

1984
Plus five handicap; South Eastern champion; member of Great Britain and Ireland team for Curtis Cup, winning single on last afternoon.

1985
Turned professional. Finished second in second event, Hennessy Cognac Ladies' Cup; won Belgian Open; won Rookie of the Year honours and European Order of Merit (prize money £21,735).

Set a new record for money won by a rookie professional.

In a long-driving contest on the eve of the Laing Classic at Stoke Poges, hit 284 yards, to be beaten only by Peter McEvoy of Amateur championship and Walker Cup fame. McEvoy drove 292 yards.

In an end-of-year interview with Michael Williams of *The Daily Telegraph*, said she had no thoughts of playing on the LPGA tour in the States, even though her winning of the Order of Merit would prompt an invitation to the 1986 US Open. Asked if she had ever believed she could win the Order of Merit in her first year as a professional, she replied, 'No way did I think I could win it.'

1986

McEwan's Wirral Classic; Greater Manchester Tournament; Weetabix British Women's Open; La Manga Club Spanish Ladies' Open. Won European Order of Merit with £37,500.

Finished 11th in her first US Open championship.

Most top ten finishes (13) along with Lotta Neumann; most rounds in the 60s (16); lowest winning total (20 under par in the Greater Manchester Open).

1987

Italian Ladies' Open; US Women's Open; second on European Order of Merit with £47,151.

First foreigner since Catherine Lacoste to win US Open.

For five days, Laura held both the Weetabix British Women's Open and the US Open titles. (She would lose the British when she finished second to Alison Nicholas at St Mellion.)

13 top ten finishes in Europe in 17 events.

Equalled record with a back nine of 29 on the last day in finishing second in French Women's Open. Created new record with a haul of 11 birdies in that same round.

1988

Circle K LPGA Tucson Open; Jamie Farr Toledo Classic; Ford Classic; Italian Ladies Open; Biarritz Ladies' Open; Itoki Classic (Japan). Played 21 tournaments in America and finished 15th on LPGA Order of Merit with $160,382. Played ten tournaments in Europe and finished eighth on European Order of Merit with £41,871.

Ambition at the start of the season had been to finish in the top ten on both sides of the Atlantic.

Had career-lowest round, a 63, on first day in Toledo.

Defeated Nancy Lopez by three shots to win the Jamie Farr.

Established new European tour record with winning total of 267 in Biarritz.

Runner-up to Lotta Neumann in LPGA's Rookie of the Year award.

1989

Lady Keystone Open; Laing Charity Classic. Played 18 tournaments in America and finished 13th on LPGA Order of Merit with $181,574. Played ten tournaments in Europe and finished 19th on European Order of Merit with £24,608.

Finished with three successive birdies to win the Lady Keystone by a shot from Pat Bradley.

1990

Biarritz Ladies' Open. Played 18 tournaments in America and finished 64th on LPGA Order of Merit. Played 11 tournaments in Europe and finished eighth on European Order of Merit with £41,871.

Highlight of Season: results in inaugural Solheim Cup. With Alison Nicholas, won opening foursome against Pat Bradley and Nancy Lopez; won single against Rosie Jones, to collect two points out of three.

1991

Valextra Classic; Inamori Classic. Played 23 tournaments in America and finished 20th on LPGA Order of Merit with £200,831. Played 12 tournaments in Europe and finished fifth on European Order of Merit with £49,552.

Ten-under-par 62 in first round of the Rail Charity Classic for a new career-lowest round. It was also a 1991 18-hole record in America.

1992

European Open; English Open; BMW Italian Open. Played 21 tournaments in America and finished 39th on LPGA Order of Merit with $150,163. Played ten tournaments in Europe and won European Order of Merit with £66,333.

Two second-place finishes in America, in the ShopRite LPGA Classic and the Rail Charity Classic and lost both on the first hole of sudden-death play-off. Anne-Marie Palli defeated her the first time; Nancy Lopez, the next.

Highlight of season: Europe's win over USA in Solheim Cup at Dalmahoy. With Alison Nicholas, won opening foursome against Betsy King and Beth Daniel, and fourball against Patty Sheehan and Julie Inkster; and won single against Brandie Burton.

1993

McDonalds Championship; Waterford Daries English Open; Thailand Open; Alpine Australian Masters. Played 16 tournaments in America to finish 20th on LPGA Order of Merit with $240,643. Played 12 tournaments in Europe and finished second on European Order of merit with £64,938.

Best financial season in the States.

Recorded a new career-lowest scoring average in the States of 72.00

1994

Standard Register Ping; Sara Lee Classic; McDonald's LPGA championship; Irish Holidays Open; New Skoda Scottish Open; Thailand Open; Itoen Ladies' Open; Alpine Australian Masters. Played 22 tournaments in America and won LPGA Order of Merit with $687,201. Played seven tournaments in Europe and finished third on European Order of Merit with £59,384.

Twelve top 10 finishes in States, including three wins and three runner-up spots.

Became 40th player in the history of the LPGA to pass the million dollar mark by virtue of her third place finish in the Health South Palm Beach Classic.

Led the Eagles tables on the LPGA tour with 15.

Recorded a new career-lowest scoring average in the States of 70.91
First player – male or female – ever to win on five different tours in the space of a single year.

First European to be ranked No.1 in the world.

First player to have hit the No.1 spot on both the European and American Orders of Merit. (European 1985, 1986 and 1992; American 1994)

1995

Standard Register Ping; Chick-Fil-A Charity Championship; Evian Masters, Guardian Irish Holidays Open, Woodpecker Welsh Open, Wilkinson Sword English Open, Itoen Ladies' Open. Played 17 tournaments in America and finished second on LPGA Order of Merit with $530,349. Played nine tournaments in Europe and finished second on European Order of Merit with £100,697.

Passed the $2 million milestone in career earnings at the Sara Lee Classic.

Won the Standard Register Ping championship for a second successive year.

1996

Standard Register Ping – hat-trick.

Satake Japan Classic

McDonalds LPGA, Dupont Country Club, Wilmington.

Evian Masters, Evian, France.

Index

Index

Index

Index